Union Rule in the Schools

Union Rule in the Schools:

Big-City Politics in Transformation

William J. Grimshaw
Illinois Institute of Technology

Lexington Books
D.C. Heath and Company
Lexington, Massachusetts
Toronto

Library of Congress Cataloging in Publication Data

Grimshaw, William J
    Union rule in the schools.

    Includes index.
    1. Education, Urban—United States. 2. Teachers' unions—United
States. I. Title.
LC5131.G74   370.19'348'0973   78-24631
ISBN 0-669-02769-3

Published simultaneously in Canada.

Printed in the United States of America.

International Standard Book Number: 0-669-02769-3

Library of Congress Catalog Card Number: 78-24631

*Dedicated to the
Memory of my Father:
straight Democratic voter,
union man to the end, and
one hell of a pool player.*

Contents

List of Figures
and Tables

Foreword

At a time when the public-employee union has become the cutting edge of the American labor movement, and cities such as New York and Cleveland teeter on the edge of bankruptcy, William Grimshaw's study of the development and consequences of union rule in Chicago schools is of major interest to scholar and citizen. It holds special interest because Mayor Richard Daley's machine was supposed to hold Chicago in its grip; and Chicago, in contrast to New York, was supposed to be a city that worked. Grimshaw's study reveals the Daley machine's Achilles heel, and pictures Daley, the tough boss, reduced to currying favor with the Union, and posturing as a mediator for publicity while sacrificing the fiscal integrity of his city that had been his pride. He does not speculate to what extent age and loss of vigor may have led Daley to a common mayoral posture, *après moi la déluge, mais après moi.* Whatever, it is some distance from the situation where Meyerson and Banfield could seriously suggest that the survival interests of the Daley machine provided a reasonably good operational definition of Chicago's public interest; a notion that Paul Peterson's account of the sober concern of the machine's establishment (labor leaders, blacks, businessmen, reformers, and all for the social and economic viability of the city) renders far from as far fetched as it once might have seemed. Grimshaw's study traces the stages through which Chicago's schools moved from machine domination through reform to the present condition of union rule. In doing so he pays his respects to Lasswell's injunction that politics is the study of who gets what, when, and how; and his three models of machine, reform and union rule make explicit both the how and the beneficiaries of the mode of governance. In none of them does he find students or parents to be a principal beneficiary in more than name, and in this the dilemma of professionals (and their clients) teachers, lawyers, or doctors is made painfully clear.

The machine domination that gripped Chicago's schools from Big Bill Thompson to Kelly was broken by scandal, giving the reformers their chance; a chance that had little to do with the strength of reform in Chicago, based as it was on the concern of middle-class Protestants and Jews with fitful media support and uncertain business support in an overwhelmingly blue-collar, ethnic, Catholic city. Yet the gods were kind; Kelly was dumped; a business reformer, Kennelly, was slated; a selection device involving civic, business, professional, welfare, labor organizations and universities to screen the mayor's choice of school board members was established; and the first of a series of outside, nationally renowned reform school superintendents was chosen. Kennelly's two terms, in which the reform mayor backed the reform superintendent to the hilt, seemed to put Chicago schools firmly in the national pattern of separation from politics. This was especially the case since Daley, despite being the machine's choice to dump Kennelly, appeared anxious to put distance between himself and the Kelly scandals, and to placate reformers and, more importantly, the business community. Thus, it was in Daley's early years that Willis's superintendency brought reform to its apogee, with insulation of schools from politics, administrative domination of teachers and well nigh the same for the school board. The schools, which had previously been run for the politicians as a source of patronage and pelf, were now run for the school administrators, and to the approval of the business constituency. By the politicians, they were no longer regarded as a tempting and available resource but as political poison that could kill you. So, sleeping dogs, at considerable cost put to sleep, might have been let lie. The reign of managerial reform might have had its lengthy day as elsewhere. But race reared its ugly head and played havoc with Daley and the machine's possibly good intentions to keep its hand out of the school cookie jar. The Superintendent and the school board could not confine the politics of school integration to the autonomous sytem of school politics. Despite deep sympathy on the part of Daley and the machine for Willis' adamant stand in support of the neighborhood schools, Willis' abrasiveness made him too great a liability for even his business allies, and another nationally known superintendent with the advantage of Chicago experience was chosen on Willis' early retirement. Gentleman Jim Redmond, however, was a conciliator, and with his entry on the scene, the dormant but always legally existent power of Daley and the machine to control the school board and the schools began to surface. Yet what transpired was not the return of machine control, but action by Daley and the machine that replaced reform rule with that of the union, and compelled Daley to ride the tiger.

The civil rights conflict explains the downfall of Willis. The escalation of the conflict beyond the confines of school politics both necessitated and provided the cover for the reentry of Daley into school politics, which had indeed become matters of burning city-wide concern. But the issues of civil rights and school integration would not seem by themselves to occasion the gift by Daley to the teachers of a power, namely that of collective bargaining, that he and the machine had fought strenuously to deny to other employees, including police and firemen. Grimshaw seems to offer as explanation the fact that Lee and the Chicago Federation of Labor, in view of the cresting importance of public-employee unions in the labor movement, had asked for it, and that a marked decline in the machine's support in the inner-city black wards lowered pluralities everywhere, and loss of assured control of primaries made new allies expedient. So in a way civil rights and race, with their impact on the machine, may have been at the bottom of Daley's abandoning his opposition to collective bargaining in the case of the teachers. Given the need for allies and the attractiveness of the teachers in that role, it must have seemed like a good gamble. Indeed, as Grimshaw relates, in the early days of moderate teachers' union leadership, everything that Daley might have hoped for was realized, and it seemed as though the teachers might become a valuable addition to the machine's docile labor allies. But, if such was the hope, it was to be rudely shattered. Within a short space of time the very moderation of the teachers' union leadership made it vulnerable to a radical faction that insisted on all and more than all the traffic would bear.

The teachers' union, having been assisted to power by Daley and the machine, proceded to go into business on its own, and not as a junior partner. Whereas under the moderate leadership the union had behaved as an ally, under the militants it drew apart, supporting its friends and opposing its enemies without regard to party affiliation. But this ingratitude on the part of the union could not be reciprocated by the Mayor. The union could push the School Board for all it was worth, and threaten the city's peace with a strike, and the best the Mayor could do was to make such points as he could by acting as a mediator between union and the Board, and by securing an expeditious settlement by forcing Board acceptance of the union's demands. Grimshaw argues that the Mayor could not have his people on the Board take a strike without being accused of union-busting, and angering his labor allies. What remains obscure is why the other public employees, seeing the teachers' success, remained quiet. Transit workers, police, firemen, and sanitation workers, as well as teachers, were not so bashful in New York and elsewhere.

The militant leaders of the Chicago teachers' union rapidly became too big for the city, and transferred their own and their members' concern from the city to the state capital and Washington, where they hoped to find the money to meet demands that were becoming clearly beyond the capacity of a school board facing mounting deficits. When asked what was Labor's platform, Samuel Gompers is reported to have answered "More." Clearly, if that were to be the unending goal of the teachers' union, the magic pitcher would have to be found, at least at the state and probably at the national level, and here it would seem but a matter of time. What Grimshaw shows is the frightening degree to which a profession with strong pretensions to serving its clients—the city's children— could, through the union device, legitimize a degree of callous selfishness that surpassed that of the managerial elite of reform, and even the rapacity of the machine. As Peterson's study of Chicago school politics shows, the businessmen, the labor leaders, the reformers (black as well as white) that made up the Chicago school board all showed some measure of common concern with the social and economic well being of the city, and to that extent they provided the city with a government that, with all its limitations, behaved responsibly. The militant union leadership accepted no responsibility except to the most narrowly selfish interests of its members. In this, its rule of the schools fits the classic definition of tyranny, a government not in the interests of the governed, but in the exclusive interests of the governors. It now remains to be seen whether the machine chosen, insider superintendent Hannon, will have the backing and the ability to tame the union. As Peterson and others have remarked, if cities are to become managements, and accord collective bargaining and the right to strike to unions, they, like private employers, will have to be willing to take strikes, an alternative to which the teachers' union would be highly vulnerable. Whether Chicago must see its machine, business, and labor establishments disintegrate, and drift into the fragmented powerlessness of New York till proximate bankruptcy calls a halt, is a question readers of this book must ponder. The rise to dominance of the public-employee union has created a force beyond the immediate discipline of the market. It has created power without accompanying responsibility, and as Grimshaw points out, has for the first time legitimized unalloyed selfishness. Unions can and have wrung the necks of geese that laid their golden eggs. Can we hope that the example of New York, where union pension funds are now invested in the city's bonds, will enlighten a selfishness that now must appear self-destructive, and teach unions that as the most powerful actors in the city they must accept a responsible part in ruling the city, and stop ruining it?

Norton E. Long
University of Missouri
St. Louis

Acknowledgments

For whatever is useful about this effort, Norton Long deserves principal credit. His careful reading and incisive comments steered me through troubled waters on more than one occasion. As many others have observed, Long is a truly gifted man. He is, in the Orwellian sense, also a good man. He writes so well in large part because he possesses a firm and sensible set of convictions, a dedication to the craft, and a genuine concern.

Paul Peterson also was a great source of help. His excellent study of Chicago's school politics and his thoughtful reading of my early efforts were helpful beyond measure. Scholars at the University of Illinois in Urbana, Phillip Monypenny, Samuel Gove, and Michael Preston, displayed patience, compassion, and grace in dealing with me and the project.

It would be remiss not to also acknowledge my political mentors. I began working in Governor Dan Walker's office full of strong conceptions about politics. Gradually and painfully I learned that politicians did and had to view matters far differently than a neophyte political scientist whose practical experience in the business had been confined to the lakefront liberal wards in Chicago. Those hard-bitten players, I think, made me a more sensible and compassionate student of politics.

Finally there is my wife, Jacky. Her passion for practicing politics must have led her to occasionally conclude that my writing-about-politics project was worth less than I supposed. Still, she endured and even helped me keep a semblance of balance by dragging me back in for one more political campaign every now and then.

All the errors are of course all my own.

1

Machine Rule, Reform Rule, and Union Rule: The Three Forms of American Big-City Government

Introduction

A fundamental transformation in big-city government occurred earlier in this century. The machine-rule form of government was replaced by the reform-rule form of government. A second transformation is occurring. Reform rule is being replaced by what may be referred to as the union-rule form of government. Union rule involves the unprecedented and increasingly influential role being played by unionized public employees in the big-city governance process, particularly within the public bureaucracies.

When the big cities were governed principally by political machines, the politicians were the dominant group in the governance process. City government under machine rule was well articulated because the politicians were able to utilize the powerful political party and a comprehensive system of patronage employment to integrally link politics and government in general and the mayor and the public bureaucracies in particular. As a result of penetration by the political party, the public bureaucracies lacked virtually any autonomy, and because of the party's patronage system of employment, the allegiance of the bureaucrats necessarily was directed primarily toward the politicians.

Accordingly, while the big cities may not have been well governed in many respects, they nevertheless were comprehensively governed, and, even more important, a substantial basis existed for achieving democratic governance. Because of the close nexus between politics and government under the machine-rule form of government, a city's citizens possessed a powerful means—the ballot—of influencing governmental policies and outcomes.

Reform rule separated politics from government. The bifurcation that was created by the reform movements in the big cities served to make the managers of the public bureaucracies a dominant group in the governance process. As Sayre and Kaufman have observed, the bureau managers became the direct beneficiaries of the decline of the big-city political party.[1] As a result of this respective waxing and waning of political influence, the big cities became disarticulated interinstitutionally. As separate spheres of autonomy began to develop, city agencies became isolated from one another, and all of the agencies more or less managed to extricate themselves from the web of influence of the political party. As the patronage system of employment waned alongside the political party, government became even further divorced from politics. For

1

the allegiance of all the bureaucrats, not merely the managers, inevitably tended to shift from the moribund political party to the newly independent and increasingly influential bureaucracy.

The legacy of reform rule is, as Theodore Lowi has pointed out, the ungovernable city.[2] With the establishment of a reform-rule form of government, the mayor is reduced from being a director of governmental outcomes to a more or less ineffectual negotiator of policy with the managers of the autonomous city bureaucracies. In turn, it can be seen that the basis for achieving democratic governance declines under the reform-rule form of government. A city's citizens still possess the ballot, enabling them to change their elected political leadership. However, because reform rule separates government from politics, a change of political leadership is no longer as likely to bring about governmental changes. The force of the reform-rule ballot often is simply incapable of penetrating the well-fortified walls constructed around the city bureaucracies by the reformers.

With the emergence of union rule, governmental changes are in the process of being separated from managerial as well as from political and citizen influence. For the leadership of the public employee unions is not elected by a city's citizens, nor is the leadership appointed by a city's elected officials or by the bureau management. The union leadership is elected solely by the union's membership, and the leadership is accountable only to the membership. The public union is, then, an autonomous sytem within other systems; however, it is a system which has considerable influence on the systems with which it interacts.

The public union's influence is the product of several factors. Once the union is granted the right to collective bargaining, the unionized employees possess a legitimate leadership role in city government. Their interests become a part of the city's political and governmental agenda. The union, in turn, is able to forcefully pursue its interests through the collective-bargaining process and through its ability to withhold public services. What cannot be gained through bargaining can be gained through coercion. Then, because it is the union which provides the bureaucrats with their benefits under a union-rule form of government, the allegiance of the city employees understandably tends to shift from the bureaucracy to the union, just as reform rule served to transfer loyalties from the political party to the bureaucracy. Thus, the union-rule bureaucrats may well regard themselves as members of private corporations, even though the public continues to foot the bills.

Reform rule produced interinstitutional disarticulation. Union rule is producing intrainstitutional disarticulation. The cities are becoming not only ungovernable but unmanageable and undemocratic as well. Union rule reduces the managers of a city's public agencies to negotiators of policy with the union leadership, much after the manner by which reform rule reduced the leadership capabilities of the mayor and other elected officials.[3]

It is not difficult to see how union rule serves to create a less democratic city as well. Since the managers appointed by a city's elected officials no longer possess the capability of determining governmental policy and outcomes without the concurrence of the union leadership, government is becoming even further divorced from politics than it was under reform rule. Union-rule politics is in the process of becoming theater. Dramatic gestures by a city's elected officials, which bear little relationship to the distribution of public values and services, to the performance of public employees, or to representative government, are becoming the new and fundamentally inadequate basis of big-city government.

Much already has been written about the transformation from machine rule to reform rule. The transformation from reform rule to union rule, on the other hand, has received far less scholarly attention.[4] Accordingly, principal attention will be directed toward the latter development. However, in order to determine in a systematic manner the most significant changes associated with the transformation to union rule and union rule's most significant dimensions, union rule will be examined within the comparative context of machine rule and reform rule, respectively. Additionally, since our thesis is that the development of union rule constitutes a major change in big-city government, the thesis will be subjected to an extremely difficult set of circumstances for the emergence and development of union rule. In this way, if the thesis holds, it is possible to infer with a higher degree of confidence that a similar development is occurring or will occur under less formidable circumstances. At the same time, by focusing on a particular set of circumstances, a detailed and comprehensive examination of union rule can be made.

The case that will be examined is the Chicago public elementary and secondary school teachers' union. Chicago represents an extremely difficult set of circumstances for the emergence and development of union rule for several reasons. Of principal importance is the fact that Chicago is the last big city still dominated by a powerful political machine. Thus, Chicago represents one end, the powerful end, of the spectrum of big-city governmental control by the political party. It is reasonable to assume that the Chicago political party would oppose the development of a union-rule form of government, and that, in any event, it possesses more power to oppose union rule than any other big-city political party.

Two factors strongly reflect, in fact, the extent to which the Chicago political party leadership does oppose union rule. The leadership of the Chicago party consistently has opposed granting collective-bargaining rights to the city's public employees, and the party leadership has been highly successful. Chicago is the only big city in the country in which the great bulk of public employees still must make do with a handshake agreement from the mayor instead of a collective-bargaining contract.[5] Securing a collective-bargaining agreement is of course a necessary precondition for the establishment of union rule.

In addition to the considerable organizational strength of the Chicago political party and the party leadership's adamant opposition to public employee collective bargaining, there is a third significant factor which militates against the development of union rule. In contrast to the great majority of big cities, Chicago has a well-established record of prudent fiscal management, and the city's economic elite work very closely with the political party leadership in maintaining the city's highly valued fiscal stability. When Mayor Richard J. Daley died, some of the city's leading businessmen sat in the back room with the city's leading politicians to designate a successor. Accordingly, it is reasonable to assume that the deficit financing and budgetary gimmickry which frequently accompany public employee collective bargaining would less likely be tolerated in Chicago than in many other major cities.

It appears evident, then, that on all three grounds the prospects for the emergence of union rule in Chicago are decidedly bleak. Thus, it is reasonable to infer that if union rule does develop under such circumstances, then the likelihood is high that union rule has developed or will develop in other big cities as well.

A public teachers' union was selected as a test for the union-rule thesis for two principal reasons. In terms of both size and expenditure, the schools invariably constitute a big city's largest public enterprise. Moreover, a city's viability is related closely to the quality of its public schools. This is because the quality of a city's manpower serves as an inducement to retain industry and attract it to the city. While a big city can of course attract manpower from beyond the city's boundaries to some extent, the city's public schools nevertheless are responsible for producing a substantial proportion of the city's labor supply. The public schools function in much the same critical manner with regard to middle-income families, either attracting them or propelling them out to the suburbs. Deficient schools constitute a loss of revenue, as well as a considerable alteration in a city's lifestyle.

The methodological reason for selecting a teachers' union for the analysis is that, like the political party, the public-school bureaucracy represents a formidable environment for the emergence and development of union rule. Fortunately for our purposes, this is as true in Chicago as elsewhere. Chicago's public schools constitute a highly reformed public bureaucracy.[6] The schools invariably are among the most reformed bureaucracies in a big city, and since union rule entails a greater or lesser degree of codetermination, it may reasonably be assumed that the school managers would be opposed to union rule. Codetermination is incompatible with the principles and practices of a highly reformed organization, and codetermination also represents a serious personal threat to the school managers, accustomed as they are to providing unilateral direction to school affairs.

Additionally, far more public concern is directed toward the public schools than toward other public bureaucracies. Earlier in the century, public outrage at the self-interested abuses of the schools by the politicians was instrumental in bringing about the reform of the public schools.[7] Today, even in cities with powerful political machines (as in Chicago), party leaders and public officials honor the taboo against political involvement in the schools. Since union rule is a high-self-interest form of government similar to machine rule, it may be expected that if the teachers' union focuses too exclusively or aggressively on the teachers' interests, then public dissatisfaction will occur, and to an extent which is greater than in the case of other less visible and less valued public bureaucracies.

Finally, it would appear that the teachers themselves represent a less fertile ground for the implantation of trade-union values and practices than employees in most other city agencies. The teachers, after all, undergo a training and socialization period in colleges and universities that is designed to inculcate in them the acceptance of the clientele of the schools as the primary beneficiary of the organization. Obviously, there is always some degree of conflict present among practitioners in organizations which seek to maintain a low level of self-interest, such as schools and hospitals. Yet, unionism presents the conflict between low and high self-interest in such stark and often dramatic terms that it would appear to require a radical reorientation in values in order for teachers to acquire a commitment to the objectives of the union and many of its activities, notably striking and picketing.[8]

Accordingly, it is again reasonable to infer that if union rule does develop in the big-city public schools, then the likelihood is high that union rule has developed or will develop in other big-city public bureaucracies as well. In the final analysis, of course, both of the inferences must be put to the test of evidence gathered in other big cities and other big-city bureaucracies.

The second respect in which the study is comparative is more specific and direct. A comparative framework for analyzing union rule will be introduced in the remaining pages of this chapter, and the same framework will be used throughout the study. Rather than examining the characteristics of union rule in isolation, union rule will be compared along a number of dimensions with the two preceding forms of urban governance, machine rule and reform rule, respectively. This approach will enable us to address the major research question that has emerged out of the "who governs" studies: what difference does it make who governs?[9] A historical comparative framework also enables us to identify changes and developments associated with union rule within a particular and concrete frame of reference. Accordingly, all three major forms of urban government can be set out in terms of their respective distinguishing characteristics, while the two fundamental transformations in big-city governance can be studied in the process.

In the remainder of this chapter, union rule will be compared to the two preceding forms of urban government along the three basic dimensions of structure, process, and characteristic set of actors involved. Distinguishing reform rule from its predecessor, machine rule, is not a difficult matter, inasmuch as a considerable number of investigations have been devoted to the subject by political scientists. However, when it comes to differentiating union rule from reform rule, it becomes necessary to turn to sociological studies for assistance. This is because political scientists have not devoted much attention to the recent transformation, nor have they developed analytic devices useful for our purposes. While sociologists have not studied public employee unionization at any length, a number of sociological concepts are well designed for such an investigation.

In chapter 2, Chicago's school politics are placed in a historical perspective. The analytic framework used to structure the history differs from conventional historical studies of the public schools in two important respects. Typically, the central focus has been upon the institutional elaboration of the educational enterprise, from which it then is inferred that considerable educational development has concomitantly occurred.[10] Here the focus will be upon who has benefited from the various ways in which the public schools historically have been structured, and to what extent the structure of the schools and the distribution of school benefits have been associated with changes in the form of city government. Thus, our central focus is broader and more political: what difference does it make who governs the city in terms of the structure of the schools and the distribution of benefits by the city's public schools?

Chapters 3, 4, and 5 are devoted to an examination of the three basic analytic dimensions of governance. Harold Lasswell's classic definition of the study of politics provides the general framework: who gets what, when, how.[11] Accordingly, chapter 3 examines the distribution of school benefits under the three major forms of city and school governance in order to determine what significant differences are associated with each of the respective forms of governance. The analysis of school policies and benefits conducted here differs from other studies of school politics in two main respects. We shall examine the broad gamut of school policies and benefits contained in the labor contracts negotiated by the school board and the teachers' union, and then compare the policies and benefits contained in the contracts with benefits obtained by the teachers during earlier periods under different forms of city government, namely machine rule and reform rule.[12]

Typically, studies of school politics are simple case studies or cross-sectional rather than longitudinal, and the studies have focused on only one or a few policies. Moreover, the policies examined often have been of a highly controversial nature, such as community control and desegregation. Such studies are not helpful in addressing the questions of what changes have occurred over time and how are school politics ordinarily conducted.

Chapter 4 takes up the question of who gets what when, which is to say, under what circumstances does union rule emerge and develop? Essentially, the investigation in this chapter centers around a proposition put forth by Edward Banfield and James Q. Wilson in their classic text on city politics. There they described the relationship between the political party and organized public employees in terms of a simple continuum of organizational strength. "Where party organization is strong, the city administration is in a relatively good position to resist the demands of the organized employees."[13]

If Banfield and Wilson are correct, we would expect to find a decline in the organizational strength of the Chicago political party which corresponds to, first, the grant of collective bargaining to the school teachers and, then, to any significant increases in benefits which subsequently are granted to the teachers. Accordingly, three well-established criteria for assessing organizational strength are used to judge the strength of the Chicago political party during the span of Mayor Daley's term. Daley assumed office in 1955 and remained in office until 1976, during which time the Chicago Teachers' Union acquired the right to collective bargaining. Thus, Daley's term of office includes the pre- and post-collective-bargaining periods, and we should find a greater and lesser degree of party strength during Daley's mayoral reign, with a significant decline occurring in the mid-1960s.

Chapter 5 examines the "how" of union rule. We shall consider the actual means by which the leadership of the political party has been able to influence school policy making in the area of teacher benefits. Four principal channels of influence into the school policy-making process will be examined for evidence of political activity and penetration. School management and school board officers are two obvious channels of political influence. School board members also constitute an important channel of influence, since most important school policies come down to a vote. A fourth important channel of political influence was created by the school reform movement in several big cities: an advisory commission for recommending school board members to the mayor. While the commissions were created for the purpose of curtailing mayoral influence on school affairs, there is of course no guarantee that commission members will not become subject themselves to mayoral influence.

Readers who are familiar with the schools and school-politics literature will recognize that in formulating such a research inquiry we are going against the grain. As Paul Peterson, a leading scholar on school politics, found following a comprehensive review of the school-politics literature, there is virtually universal agreement concerning a central tenet about the schools: "School policy-formation is conducted autonomously by specialists in the field who are virtually impervious to pressure from external sources."[14] What we would expect to find, however, is that such a high degree of autonomy may be characteristic of school politics during the reform-rule period, but not as much autonomy would obtain during the union-rule period, and hardly any autonomy would be found during the earlier machine-rule period. In other words, the conventional wisdom about the autonomy of the schools is predicated on the schools being operated as a reform organization. Union rule, however, serves to alter the schools in a number of significant ways, including subjecting them to a renewal of external political influence.

Finally, chapter 6 is devoted to a consideration of the several propositions associated with the proposed union-rule model of big-city governance. The model is evaluated in terms of its applicability—how well does the model "fit" the empirical situation we have examined?—and in terms of its utility—for what purposes is the union-rule model useful?

The First Great Transformation:
From Machine Rule to Reform Rule

Much already has been written concerning the transformation from the machine-rule form of government to the reform-rule form of government in American big cities. Only a brief outline of the major dimensions of the transformation is therefore required in order to place the subsequent transformation to union rule in sufficient context. General agreement can be found in the urban-politics literature that what is considered to be the reform-rule form of urban government involves three interrelated government dimensions. Reform rule is said to differ from its predecessor, machine rule, in terms of the way in which government is structured, the processes by which government is conducted, and the set of actors who characteristically carry out governmental activities.

The structure of reform government invariably is described as being significantly more decentralized and disarticulated than machine rule. In a seminal analysis, Norton Long described local government as consisting of an "ecology of games," to the effect that the city is lacking not only a unity of command, but unity of purpose as well.[15] The description that Wallace Sayre and Herbert Kaufman provide of New York City's governmental structure is in many respects a detailed extension of Long's observations. Government there is said to consist of a "multiplicity of decision-centers." In rich detail, Sayre and Kaufman point out the numerous perils and contradictions associated with a multicentered system of governmental structure.[16] Even Edward Banfield's description of Chicago's governmental structure, notwithstanding the presence of the powerful political party, contains similar observations about the decentralization of government. Banfield found such a number of power and influence centers in Chicago that critical outcomes perforce required compromises if stalemates were to be avoided.[17]

A second point of general agreement involves the observation that a reform-rule form of government is significantly more efficient, honest, and rooted in rational principles and procedures than its machine-rule predecessor. The fountainhead of such observations, of course, is Max Weber. Weber identified efficiency, honesty, and rationality as critical characteristics of the modern bureaucracy, and bureaucratic dominance is closely associated with the reform-rule form of urban government.[18] In Theodore Lowi's terms, "The legacy of Reform is the bureaucratic state." According to Lowi, "The decentralization of city government toward its career bureaucracies has resulted in great efficiency for the activities around which each bureaucracy was organized. The city is indeed well run."[19] Urban scholars Edward Banfield and James Q. Wilson also have characterized modern government in similar terms. While denying the causal significance of reform measures, the authors nevertheless agree that "City government is vastly more honest, efficient, and democratic than it was a generation or two ago."[20]

The third point of general agreement found in the urban-politics literature is that the set of actors characteristically associated with a reform-rule form of government differs in a number of critical respects from their machine-rule counterparts. The reform-rule bureaucrats are more neutral in regard to partisan politics, more committed to the norms and needs of a particular functional affiliation, and more inclined to regard external attempts to influence the activities of the bureaucracy, whether they emanate from above or below, as illegitimate.

Together, these viewpoints may be said to summarize the outlook of the professional bureaucrat. Again, the seminal source of the observations is Max Weber's studies of the modern bureaucracy. In examining New York City politics and government, Theodore Lowi observed just this type of transformation in outlook as reform rule began to replace machine rule. The last leaders of the declining Tammany political machine, Carmine DeSapio and Edward Costikyan, were, in effect, bridges to the new reform point of view. "Each was progressively more public-regarding than any of his predecessors. Costikyan was a model of political responsibility for whom the new New York had no particular use." Subsequently, as reform rule became more firmly established, Lowi observed an even more marked change in the viewpoint of the bureaucrats. The "Bosses of the New Machines—the bureau chiefs and the career commissioners—will be loyal to their agency, its work, and related professional norms."[21]

As for the bureaucrats whom the reform chiefs and commissioners direct, after examining a number of different city governments, Edward Banfield was inclined to attribute the increased honesty and competence he had found in the governmental agencies to the presence of more reform bureaucrats in these agencies. "The presence of large numbers of professionals, whose tenure is made secure by merit systems, probably accounts to a large extent for the greater honesty and competence of the city governments."[22] The tenure system and other protective features of reform apparently better enabled the bureaucrats to withstand external attempts to influence their behavior along less honest and competent lines.

In addition to identifying those areas where general agreement can be found in the urban-politics literature, it also is important to note that several serious omissions can be found in the same literature. The omissions are of considerable significance in that an important dimension of the transformation from machine rule to reform rule is slighted, if not altogether ignored. Not enough attention is focused on the enhanced potential for change or on changes that actually occurred in the bureaucracies once they acquired a position of autonomy and dominance under reform rule.[23] Three major problems stemming from these shortcomings will be addressed here.

First, there has been a serious oversight in the urban-politics literature at the level of elites in the political system. The shortcoming involves the failure to properly focus attention in keeping with the shift from machine to reform rule. As James Q. Wilson has observed, it is ironic and unfortunate that when

power and influence were concentrated informally and extralegally within the
political party, political scientists generally were focusing their attention on the
formal, legal elites and institutions. Then, to make matters worse, when power
and influence shifted under reform rule toward the elites and institutions that
political scientists had been examining, political scientists began to shift their
attention elsewhere. The new focus of inquiry generally became the informal
and extralegal components of government. The large volume of "who governs"
literature developed during the 1960s exemplifies the new emphasis by urban-
oriented political scientists.[24]

This is not to deny the enduring significance of extralegal and informal
elites and institutions in politics, but only to say that, under a reform-rule form
of government, they are relatively less significant. In any event, a good deal more
attention should be devoted to the reform-rule elites, the bureaucratic leadership, and their institutional setting, the modern bureaucracy. This would enable
us, for example, to more adequately evaluate Theodore Lowi's provocative
characterization of the modern bureaucracies as the "new Machines" and their
professional managers as the "new Bosses." As things stand, the urban-politics
literature provides scant aid.[25] No less important, the literature leaves largely
unaddressed the critical question of what difference it makes whether a city is
governed by old or new bosses and machines.

The second shortcoming in the literature that we shall consider occurs at the
level of citizens in the political system. Related to the preoccupation with informal and extralegal elites and institutions is a particular methodology used to
analyze them. In determining who the major governors were, the predominant
research strategy involved analyzing the central issues confronting a city. On
purely methodological grounds, there is merit to such an approach. If one has it
in mind to determine who wields power and influence, it makes sense to observe
the wielders in action. Presuming one step further, should one seek to identify
the biggest wielders, then one ought to look to where the biggest action is
occurring. This usually will direct one's attention to where the big changes are
occurring or being attempted.[26]

However, this reasoning suggests the substantive shortcoming of the conventional methodology. For what Dahl, Banfield, and others using the approach
have done is, in effect, to equate governance with the regulation of change.
Change is what the big issues center around. Change, however, is not what
government centers around. From the viewpoint of a government's significant
impact on a city's citizens, change constitutes an occasional and often minor
aspect of government. Accordingly, by identifying a city's chief change agents
as its governors, the literature ignores the bulk of city governmental activities,
the elites who govern these activities, and the relationships among the activities
of these elites and the broad range of regularly occurring outcomes that are
produced.

In contrast, then, to the issue-focused and change-oriented approach, what is required is an institution-focused and maintenance-oriented type of analysis. For it is through a city's bureaucracies that the significant elites function, and function in a regular and substantial manner with a city's citizens. Moreover, it is the outputs of a city's primary maintenance bureaucracies, such as health care, education, and public safety, which comprise the substance of government and which matter most to the quality of life of a city's citizens.[27]

The third shortcoming occurs at the level of the public bureaucracies. The problem here stems from a failure to consider the actual changes and vastly increased potential for change which came about as a result of the reformation of the bureaucracies. The marvelous vision of many of the early reformers concerning the changes that reform of the bureaucracies would produce hinged upon a critical supposition: that politics would be eliminated and that consequently the bureaucracies would function in a value-neutral manner. The modern bureaucracy would operate autonomously of the city's politics, and the bureaucracy would be managed and manned by professionals possessing no politics in their calculus.[28]

The urban-politics literature has supplied several significant corrections to the optimistic viewpoint of the early reformers. Yet, it is important to recognize that these corrections apply essentially to the external politics of the bureaucracy. Thus, the literature has pointed out the crucial fact that the autonomy of the modern bureaucracy has been partially penetrated by its need to go outside the agency for funding. Accordingly, it is said, on the one hand, that the modern bureaucracy "shapes important public policy" and that it is "not readily subject to the controls of any higher authority."[29] However, on the other hand, it takes money to continue setting policy, and politicians beyond the bureaucracy hold the purse. This has led Edward Banfield, for example, to conclude that bureau managers wind up more resembling Max Weber's ideal-type politician than his ideal-type bureaucrat, as they seek to wind their way successfully through the highly political appropriations process.[30]

Another source of penetration into the autonomous modern bureaucracy has been identified by Theodore Lowi: the politicans' need for electoral and administrative support in a time of declining party organizational strength.[31] Based on an assessment of developments in New York City during the early 1960s, Lowi perceives relations between the politicians and the bureaucrats as having become so intimate that two political hybrids have been produced: the ex-bureau commissioner as party leader and the bureaucracy as the new political clubhouse. According to Lowi, the logic and political necessity inherent in the developments are sufficiently compelling to indicate that New York's fate could well be the fate of other big-city reform governments.

As the analysis goes, the basic needs of a city's elected officials, particularly the mayor, are an electoral base with which to get elected, and once elected, a basis for achieving effective and coordinated governmental action. However, the powerful political clubhouses, which used to serve both functions, no longer exist—hence the compelling impetus for creating the novel hybrids. The transformed bureaucracies will organize and supply the votes, as the party clubhouses once were able to do. The politicized ex-bureau commissioners will serve as party leaders in order to generate a supportive vote from the bureaucrats, and, following the election, they will produce the coordinated governmental action that the clubhouse bosses once were capable of supplying.

Lowi's analysis, though certainly provocative, is not altogether convincing. As far as it goes, his treatment of the external politics of the reform bureaucracy is reasonable. But Lowi seriously misconstrues the internal structure and politics of the bureaucracy. He appears to have basically accepted the early reformist view of the internal workings of the bureaucracy. The early reformers characterized the bureaucracy as an efficient, hierarchical, and well-articulated organization, much like a machine. Lowi, in fact, describes the bureaucracies as the "new Machines." In comparing the bureaucracies to the old machines, the political parties, Lowi maintains the bureaucracies are "more monolithic by far than their ancient brethren."[32]

Yet, even as Lowi's description was being written, the bureaucracies were undergoing a major, multifaceted transformation. The essence of the transformation is that the autonomy which the modern bureaucracies had acquired and the unilateral authority possessed by the bureau leadership are being substantially reduced by the burgeoning public employee unions. The unilateral managerial authority of the bureau leadership appointed by the mayor is being sharply and widely curtailed by contracts negotiated with the labor unions. The functional autonomy of the bureaucracies is being breached through employee affiliations with powerful, self-interested labor unions. The monolithic structure of the bureaucracy is being fundamentally severed by the establishment of formal and highly influential distinctions between labor and management rights. The professionalism of the bureaucrat is now commingling with his unionism. Thus, bureaucracies are underoing a major transformation, but in a direction different from that indicated by Lowi's analysis.

The Second Great Transformation:
From Reform Rule to Union Rule

The critical outcome of reform rule is that the big cities have become ungovernable. With the transformation to union rule, the big cities are in the process of becoming unmanageable and undemocratic as well. When we distinguished reform rule from machine rule, the three basic categories of structure, process, and set of actors were used. Accordingly, the same categories will be used to compare reform rule and union rule. However, inasmuch as political scientists have not devoted much attention to what we are calling union rule, it will be necessary to draw more heavily upon concepts developed by sociologists for the analysis presented in this section.

The distinguishing structural characteristic of a reform-rule form of urban government is interinstitutional disarticulation. The distinctive structural feature of a union-rule form of big-city government is intrainstitutional disarticulation. The intrainstitutional disarticulation does not, however, displace the interagency disjunction characterizing reform rule. Thus, in addition to the overlay of disarticulation among public agencies, a lack of articulation also is developing within the agencies of big-city government. Not only has the mayor's office lost much of its ability to influence management, but management is losing much of its ability to influence labor. Accordingly, the classic tradeoff between governmental power and responsiveness becomes irrelevant under union rule.[33] A union-rule form of government is neither powerful nor responsive, except insofar as the interests of the membership of the public employee unions are concerned.

It was possible to distinguish four hierarchical and articulated levels of governmental structure much more clearly prior to union rule than after its establishment. At the primary level of government, technical activities and responsibilities are carried out. Teachers in a public school system, patrolmen in a police department, and doctors in a public health agency, for example, perform at the technical level of government.

The next higher level is managerial. The primary internal responsibility at this level is the control and supervision of employees at the technical level. A distinctively higher order of governmental organization, control, and responsibility exists at the institutional level. This level may be distinguished primarily by its responsibility for articulating the organization with the broader, citywide system of government. This level of organization characteristically consists of a lay board, such as a board of education. The distinctive difference between the managerial and institutional levels is well reflected by the fact that recruitment to the institutional level is made from the city-at-large, rather than from within the organization in question.

The city's most comprehensive level of governmental organization is the political level. Talcott Parsons characterizes the political level by a threefold set of responsibilities: the allocation of values and resources, the articulation of the area's public institutions, and "supplying" binding decisions in response to citizen "demands." The capability of the actors at the political level in meeting their responsibilities depends largely upon the extent to which the city's governmental structure is hierarchically structured and articulated.[34]

Accordingly, it can be seen that the development of a union-rule form of city government constitutes a radical transformation in governmental authority structure. Under union rule, the four levels of governmental organization are no longer as distinct, hierarchical, or articulated. What union rule critically entails is the assumption by the actors at the technical level of rights, responsibilities, and control which previously had been held by actors at each of the three super-ordinate governmental levels.

Managerial control and discretion are sharply and widely curtailed by the articles of agreement contained in the collective-bargaining contracts reached by the leadership of the institutional and technical levels. The capability of the institutional-level actors is diminished to the extent that the technical level is able to establish the principles and practices of codetermination. The political-level actors, in turn, lose their control over the organization, and they give up allocational and decision-making authority on a citywide basis to the extent that the institutional level relinquishes its unilateral authority. Decisions made, then, at the political level will possess little likelihood of implementation, except insofar as they are compatible with the interests of the unionized actors at the technical level of government.

In terms of governmental process, the transformation to union rule is no less radical. In order to illustrate the nature of the transformation from reform rule to union rule, it is useful to draw upon a typology of formal organizations developed by sociologists Peter Blau and W. Richard Scott. Blau and Scott used the primary beneficiary of an organization as the basis for identifying four basic types of organizations. Table 1-1 developed from Blau and and Scott's analysis, indicates the usefulness of the four-fold typology for our purposes.

Our interest centers on two of the four organizational types developed by Blau and Scott. One of these, mutual-benefit associations, is characterized as a high-self-interest type of organization, which has as its primary beneficiary the membership of the association. The other organizational type of interest is the service organization. In contradistinction to a mutual-benefit association, a service organization is a low-self-interest type of organization, which is geared to

Table 1-1
A Typology of Formal Organizations Based upon Prime Beneficiary

Organizational Type	Prime Beneficiary	Examples
High Self-Interest		
Mutual-benefit associations	Membership	Political parties, professional associations, unions
Business concerns	Owners	industrial firms, banks, stores
Low Self-Interest		
Service organizations	Clients	Schools, social welfare agencies, hospitals
Commonweal organizations	Public-at-large	Police, fire, military

Source: Peter M. Blau and W. Richard Soctt, Formal Organizations: A Comparative Approach (San Francisco: Chandler Publishing Co., 1962), pp. 40-58.

serving the clientele of the organization, rather than the organization's practitioners. Accordingly, when the two organizational types coexist within an organization, as in the case of a teachers' union within a public school system, conflict is likely to occur over the identity of the organization's prime beneficiary. Is it to be the organization's clientele or the union's membership?

Blau and Scott addressed this kind of question in developing their typology. First, they considered a form of conflict which is inherent in service organizations, regardless of whether a union exists within the organization.

> The crucial problems of these organizations center around providing professional services. . . . In the typical case, however, the client does not know what will best serve his own interest. . . . Hence, the client is vulnerable, subject to exploitation, and dependent on the integrity of the professional to whom he has come for help.[35]

A second-order problem occurs when the practitioners resolve the conflict for themselves in the direction of serving their own self-interest.

> In service organizations, if the members of the professional staff lose interest in serving clients and become primarily concerned with making their own work easier or furthering their own careers, service will suffer, since the energy and resources devoted to it will no longer be considered as contributing to the prime function of the organization but rather as a necessary cost for obtaining benefits for the staff or some segment of it.[36]

Given this groundwork laid by Blau and Scott, it is apparent that there are two problems facing a service organization whose professional practitioners are granted the right to collective bargaining. To begin with, the conferral of collective-bargaining rights serves to significantly reduce the tension felt by many professional practitioners between serving their own self-interest and the interests of the organization's clientele. For the grant of collective bargaining legitimizes the right of the practitioners to pursue their own self-interest and to restructure the organization so that their self-interests are better served. The grant of collective bargaining is an acknowledgement that the practitioners are a significant, if not necessarily the primary, beneficiary of the organization.

Once collective bargaining is granted and the professional practitioners are provided with a legitimate right to pursue their self-interests within the framework of a service organization's other purpose, that of serving client interests, the critical question becomes how the two objectives are reconciled: how can the service organization's formal leadership, the lay board and management, as well as the city's formal leadership, elected public officials, maintain the values and behavior associated with low self-interest among the organization's unionized professional practitioners?

According to the sociologist Amitai Etzioni, there are essentially three means by which any organization can get its practitioners to comply with the goals of the organization.[37] Organizations may rely upon monetary rewards to gain compliance. In this instance, practitioners who meet the objectives of the organization more successfully than others are rewarded more favorably. Organizations also may rely upon coercion to gain compliance. Here, of course, sanctions must be available so that practitioners who deviate from the organization's objectives can be brought into compliance. Finally, an organization can more or less exclusively recruit members who have undergone extensive periods of professional training and socialization that have been geared toward developing a commitment to the organization's goals. This strategy amounts to a form of self-policing and policing by peers, a compliance pattern common to professional practitioners, such as medical doctors and lawyers. In practice, organizations can and do rely upon various combinations and variations of these three forms of compliance.

Yet, what is important to recognize for our purposes is that unionization serves to diminish the effectiveness as well as the legitimacy of all three compliance structures. Unions invariably oppose the distribution of differential monetary rewards based on merit, preferring to distribute benefits on the basis of seniority. Unions of the craft, professional, and semiprofessional type also are opposed to coercive types of compliance structures, preferring forms of codetermination or even unilateral control by the union. Thus, this leaves self-policing as the form of compliance favored by unions of the craft, professional, and semiprofessional type. The problem, however, is that whenever the interests of the union membership and the clientele of the organization are in conflict, it is unreasonable to except the union's leadership to support the clientele's interests over the membership's interests, or to expect the membership of the union to support altruistic leadership behavior. The purpose of the union is to advance membership interests; it is management's responsibility to look after client interests.

The final comparison that we shall make between reform rule and union rule involves some of the significant characteristics typically found among the actors occupying the bureaucracies under the two different forms of urban governance. Earlier we observed that reform-rule bureaucrats could be distinguished from their machine-rule counterparts along three interrelated dimensions. Reform-rule bureaucrats characteristically are more neutral politically, more committed to the norms and needs of a particular functional affiliation, and more inclined to regard external attempts to influence their behavior as illegitimate.

These distinctive attributes were characterized as typifying the outlook of the reform-rule bureaucrat. Of course, in practice the bureaucrat generally was unable to perform along such unadulterated professional lines. Nevertheless, reform rule's opposition to the patronage system of employment, its protective civil-service code and merit system of advancement, and its distinction between politics and administration did serve to attract and produce from within the bureaucracy a set of actors who characteristically possessed markedly different attributes from their machine-rule predecessors.

Using the same three criteria to compare union-rule bureaucrats with reform-rule bureaucrats, it once again can be seen that the transformation to union rule constitutes a radical departure from the past. In terms of the political-involvement criterion, the neutrality characterizing the typical reform-rule bureaucrat gives way to the union-rule bureaucrat's open commitment to political partisanship and activity. Reform rule's sacred taboo against the intermingling of politics and government is clearly regarded by the union-rule bureaucrats as a naïve artifact of an unproductive past. As union leaders are fond of putting it, the bureaucrats now engage in collective bargaining rather than collective begging, and the union engages in a number of activities to gain political support for its interests.

"Scorecards" are maintained by unions which rank elected officials on the basis of how well they have supported issues dear to the union's interests. In newspapers and election materials published by a union, the membership is strongly urged to vote only for those elected officials who have "earned" the union's support. As well, a portion of the union membership's dues frequently is earmarked specifically for political activities. The funds, along with whatever manpower support a union can provide, make the union a significant political force, particularly at a time when political parties have become less effective electoral-support mechanisms. Finally, a segment of a union's staff usually is assigned duties of a more or less exclusively political nature. Such individuals are employed mainly as lobbyists on the union's behalf; but, again with the decline of the political-party structure, union organizers can play vital campaign roles by virtue of their political expertise and political and union connections.

The reform-rule bureaucrat's commitment to the norms and needs of a particular functional affiliation also is undergoing a sharp change with the emergence of the union-rule bureaucrat. Essentially, the transformation involves a more encompassing commitment, which includes a union affiliation as well as a bureau affiliation. The affiliation to a union extends a bureaucrat's orientation in two ways: horizontal as well as vertical interests and ties are formed.

Vertically, a local union usually will possess an affiliation with a broader state-level union, with an even broader national-level union, and in most instances there is also an affiliation with the AFL-CIO. Thus, for example, a school teacher in Chicago is represented locally by the Chicago Teachers' Union, at the state level by the Illinois Federation of Teachers, nationally by the American Federation of Teachers, and by the AFL-CIO. Reinforcing these ties, the Chicago school teacher will learn through the union's monthly newspaper that his union president also is the president of the state union, an influential vice-president of the national union, and a delegate to the AFL-CIO. Accordingly, the union newspaper carries coverage of events at the state and national levels, as well as the local level, which involve the Chicago teachers' interests. Using Robert Merton's conceptual framework, the union serves to create cosmopolitans out of locals, and for many once-lowly public servants, this must be a heady transformation indeed.

Broader horizontal ties also are brought about through participation in a union. Such ties may be of a formal as well as an informal nature. A formal tie may be created through formal union mergers within and across functional lines. The most notable instance of this type of activity is occurring in the recruitment activities of the American Federation of State, County, and Municipal Employees' Union. AFSCME recruits union members along functional rather than agency lines. Thus, for example, all of the clerical workers in a city's government may be affiliated with AFSCME, while being employed in any one of several different public bureaucracies. The clerks, in turn, will discover that they have interests in common not only with all of the city's public clerks, but also with all the other types of city employees represented by AFSCME. Again, it is not difficult to conceive that this may well represent an intoxicating change. For those at the bottom of the governmental employment pole, often regarded as little more than mere appendages of the machines they operate (typewriters, brooms, or whatever), to be able to bring the mayor of the city to the bargaining table and perhaps to his knees as well is the stuff of which dreams are made.

Horizontal ties of an informal nature can be formed through supportive actions during times of duress involving different functional types of unions. "An injury against one is an injury against all" is the union adage dictating this type of supportive activity. Honoring the picket lines of fellow union members on strike is the most commonplace activity in this category. Different unions also can and do form horizontal ties for electoral efforts. Thus, for example, the Chicago Teachers' Union has participated in the All-Chicago Labor Committee, a citywide organization of labor unions formed primarily to support candidates from the regular Democratic party.[38] Finally, during times of extreme duress, unions may even go out on strike in an effort to support the strike efforts of another union.

The final way in which we shall distinguish the union-rule bureaucrat from his reform-rule predecessor represents in certain respects the most significant difference. The reform-rule bureaucrat tended to regard efforts to influence his behavior which emanated from sources external to the bureaucracy as illegitimate. This meant, on the one hand, that the clientele of the organization could not serve as a legitimate source of influence. Clients of course possess preferences; however, they cannot express objective interests. According to the fondest analogy of professionals and semiprofessionals: patients and their families do not dictate to the physician.

Politicians also are regarded by the reform-rule bureaucrat as an illegitimate source of influence. The politicians' lack of specialized training, expert knowledge, and dispassionate neutrality place them well beyond the pale of professional credibility. However, in view of the practical fact that politicians, unlike clients, possess considerable and even legally sanctioned influence over many bureau activities, the bureaucrats cannot fend off politicans as readily as clients. Thus, bureaucrats acquiesce and finesse as well as they can, resigning themselves to the inevitability of the occasional democratic incursion into the professional world of the bureaucracy from the political side.

Union-rule bureaucrats do not differ in this regard from their reform-rule counterparts. Union rule differs in its commitment to extend the scope of illegitimacy one highly significant step further. Union rule extends the scope of illegitimate influence over bureaucratic affairs so that it also encompasses unilateral managerial influence and authority. Union rule in effect creates an autonomous place for the professional practitioners within the broader bureaucratic structure by replacing managerial authority with contractual authority. Management's authority is further reduced inasmuch as the contractual terms governing the organization are drawn up principally by the leadership of the technical and institutional levels. Management's role in the negotiations determining its place in the organization's authority structure is advisory and at the discretion of the institutional level.

Extending the definition of illegitimate influence to include unilateral managerial authority may be viewed as an extension of the basic opposition to lay influence by professional practitioners. Management obviously is not a lay body in the same sense as clientele and politicians. It is a lay body, however, in the more fundamental sense that the managers are not expert practitioners.

In view of the tremendous increases in organizaticnal technology and knowledge which have been developed in recent years, the demands by the technical level for increased decision-making authority and less managerial supervision obviously possess considerable merit. Indeed, the argument of the practitioners for increased participation in the authority structure of organizations has received widespread support from scholars in recent years. Students of formal organizations increasingly reject the traditional models of bureaucratic authority and convincingly argue that the fundamental problem of the modern bureaucracy is the growing imbalance between formal authority and ability in the organization.[39]

The solution, proposed by practitioners and academics alike, is to bring down the traditional hierarchical authority structure of the organization, and to replace it with a wide range of decision-making procedures housed at the technical levels of the organization. This brings authority and ability into congruence. The problem with such a solution, however, is that when the expert practitioners become unionists as well, there are few means left by which to assure that the experts will serve the clients' and the public's interests rather than their own.

Notes

1. Wallace S. Sayre and Herbert Kaufman, *Governing New York City* (New York: W.W. Norton & Co., 1965).

2. Theodore J. Lowi, "Gosnell's Chicago Revisited via Lindsey's New York," foreword to the second edition, in Harold F. Gosnell, *Machine Politics: Chicago Model* (Chicago: University of Chicago Press, 1968).

3. "Managers" here is being used in the broader sense to include governing board members as well as the professional management of the organization.

4. In a literal sense, union rule has received no scholarly attention, since we are introducing the concept. Practically speaking, however, the unionization of public employees has received only scant attention from political scientists, and the majority of political scientists who have addressed the subject have confined their attention mostly to the fiscal consequences of public employee unionization. Thus, the only one of the major "who governs" studies to accord attention to the influence of the public employee organizations and unions was Sayre and Kaufman's *Governing New York City*. Other political scientists who have studied public employee unions generally have concluded that the unions' attention has been mainly confined to salary and related considerations. See, for example, in regard to teachers' unions, Marilyn Gittell, "Professionalism and Public Participation in Educational Policy-Making: New York City, A Case Study," *Public Administration Review* 27 (September 1967), and for police unions, Margaret Levi, *Bureaucratic Insurgency* (Lexington, Mass.: Lexington Books, D.C. Heath, 1977). However, some political scientists have discerned far greater aspirations in the public employee unions and observed that the unions created far more than fiscal consequences for the city. These studies emphasize the political, organizational, and public-policy influences the public unions are acquiring and have acquired. See, for example, Alan Rosenthal, "Pedagogues and Power," *Urban Affairs Quarterly* 2 (September 1966), pp. 83-102. Rosenthal's study is fascinating in that he observed a set of teachers' unions just at the point when some of them were shifting their attention from the salary issue to broader policy areas. Herbert Kaufman observed a similar development in the New York City public employee unions which he had examined earlier with Wallace Sayre. See Herbert Kaufman, "Bureaucrats and Organized Civil Servants," in Robert H. Connery and Demetrios Caraley, eds., *Governing the City: Challenges and Options for New York* (New York: Praeger Publications, 1969), pp. 41-54. On the political and organizational influence of public employee unions in general, see Sterling Spero and John M. Capozzola, *The Urban Community and Its Unionized Bureaucracies: Pressure Politics in Local Government Labor Relations* (New York: Dunellen, 1973). Thus, at this level of analysis, our study addresses the debate: how influential are the public unions, and how broad is the scope of their influence?

5. Teachers at the junior-college and elementary and secondary levels have secured collective-bargaining rights. However, the police, fire, sanitation, clerical and other public employee groups have yet to acquire collective-bargaining rights.

6. Joseph Pois, *The School Board Crisis: A Chicago Case Study* (Chicago: Educational Methods, 1964). Paul E. Peterson, *School Politics: Chicago Style* (Chicago: University of Chicago Press, 1976).

7. For the general change, see Joseph M. Cronin, *The Control of Urban Schools: Perspective on the Power of Educational Reformers* (New York: Free Press, 1973). For Chicago in particular, see Mary J. Herrick, *The Chicago Schools: A Social and Political History* (Beverly Hills, Cal.: Sage Publications, 1971).

8. The American Federation of Teachers did not repeal its opposition to teacher strikes until its 1963 annual convention. The much more conservative National Education Association finally adopted a more militant stance in response to the AFT's organizing successes in a number of big cities.

9. James Q. Wilson first raised the question. See his introductory remarks in James Q. Wilson, ed., *City Politics and Public Policy* (New York: John Wiley and Sons, 1968).

10. James S. Coleman and his associates devastated the conventional inference in the so-called Coleman Report. James S. Coleman, et al., *Equality of Educational Opportunities* (Washington, D.C.: Office of Education, 1966).

11. Harold D. Lasswell, *Politics: Who Gets What, When, How* (New York: McGraw-Hill Book Co., 1936).

12. A disproportionate number of school-politics studies are of the case-study variety and even those of a comparative nature remain at the cross-sectional level. For a comprehensive bibliographical essay, see Frederick M. Wirt's in Michael W. Kirst, ed., *State, School, and Politics: Research Directions* (Lexington, Mass.: Lexington Books, D.C. Heath, 1972). Wirt recently has demonstrated the fruitfulness of examining school politics in a historical context while using a much broader range of variables than is customarily provided. See Frederick M. Wirt, "Policy as Value, Region, and History in the American States: The Case of Education," paper prepared for delivery at the Midwest Political Science Association Annual Convention, Chicago, April 1978.

13. Edward Banfield and James Q. Wilson, *City Politics* (New York: Vintage Books, 1963), p. 214.

14. Paul E. Peterson, "The Politics of American Education," in Fred Kerlinger and John Carroll, eds., *Review of Research in Education, Vol. II* (Itasca, Ill.: Peacock, 1974).

15. Norton E. Long, "The Local Community as an Ecology of Games," *American Journal of Sociology* 44 (November 1958), pp. 251–261.

16. Sayre and Kaufman, *Governing New York City*.

17. Edward Banfield, *Political Influence: A New Theory of Urban Politics* (New York: Free Press, 1961).

18. Max Weber, *From Max Weber: Essays in Sociology,* trans. and ed. by H.H. Gerth and C. Wright Mills (New York: Oxford University Press, 1946).

19. Lowi, "Gosnell's Chicago," pp. ix, xiii.

20. Banfield and Wilson, *City Politics,* p. 149.

21. Lowi, "Gosnell's Chicago," pp. xvi, xi.

22. Edward Banfield, *Big City Politics* (New York: Random House, 1965), p. 14.

23. The notable exception is Sayre and Kaufman, *Governing New York City.*

24. Wilson, *Politics and Policy.*

25. Lowi, "Gosnell's Chicago."

26. The most influential proponents of this approach have been Edward Banfield, *Political Influence,* and Robert Dahl, *Who Governs?* (New Haven, Conn.: Yale University Press, 1961).

27. Two recent studies with such a focus have been conducted by Frank S. Levy, Arnold J. Meltzner, and Aaron Wildavsky, *Urban Outcomes: Schools, Streets, and Libraries* (Berkeley: University of California Press, 1974), and by Robert L. Lineberry, *Equality and Urban Policy: The Distribution of Municipal Public Services* (Beverly Hills, Cal.: Sage Publications, 1977).

28. Sheldon S. Wolin provides an excellent analysis of the reform point of view in "The Age of Organization and the Sublimation of Politics," chapter 10 in his *Politics and Vision: Continuity and Innovation in Western Political Thought* (Boston: Little, Brown & Co., 1960).

29. Lowi, "Gosnell's Chicago," p. x.

30. Banfield, *Political Influence,* p. 266.

31. Lowi, "Gosnell's Chicago."

32. Ibid., p. xi.

33. James Q. Wilson has written, "American local government clearly faces the same dilemma of democratic government generally—that of coping with the trade-off between a capacity for innovation and a sensitivity to citizen interests." *Politics and Policy,* p. 13.

34. The preceding discussion of levels of government structure draws on Talcott Parsons, "General Theory in Sociology," in Robert K. Merton, et al., eds., *Sociology Today* (New York: Harper Torchbooks, 1959), pp. 4–16.

35. Peter M. Blau and W. Richard Scott, *Formal Organizations: A Comparative Approach* (San Francisco: Chandler Publishing Co., 1962), p. 51.

36. Ibid., p. 42.

37. Amitai W. Etzioni, *A Comparative Analysis of Complex Organizations* (New York: Free Press, 1961).

38. *Chicago Union Teacher* (a monthly newspaper published by the Chicago Teachers' Union), February 1971.

39. An early and influential statement of such a viewpoint is contained in Victor A. Thompson, *Modern Organizations: A General Theory* (New York: Alfred A. Knopf, 1961).

2 The Beneficiaries of Chicago's Public Schools in a Historical Perspective

Introduction

Histories of the public schools have tended to treat the schools in terms of stages of progressive development and expansion. One problem with such an approach has been identified by the educational historian Michael Katz: "the common word 'expansion' implies an evolutionary, teleological process, increments of the same piled on top of one another."[1] An equally serious problem is the crucial inference that typically is contained in the histories. The studies elaborate a number of institutional developments, such as increases in the number of texts and teaching methods, a vastly expanded array of instructional and supportive services and personnel, improved physical facilities, and the like. The reader is thereby encouraged to conclude that the educational opportunities of the school systems' clientele have improved correspondingly.

Several studies in recent years have not been content to let the conventional inference rest. Rather than focusing on educational inputs, these studies have examined the actual productivity of the schools.[2] By shifting the focus of analysis, the debunkers arrived at two remarkable conclusions. The productivity of the public schools is overwhelmingly low, and school productivity is not related in any significant way to the full array of institutional factors. Recent inquiries of a historical nature on the productivity of the big-city public schools have turned up, if less precisely, essentially similar results.[3]

The conclusion, then, is dismal indeed. The current inability of the big-city public schools to meet the needs of the majority of their clientele is fundamentally no different than their historical failure with a succession of European immigrants to the big city. Today's black children fare hardly any better than yesterday's immigrant children, notwithstanding the abundance of institutional changes which have taken place in the schools over the years. Our big-city schools, in short, have been consistently unsuccessful public enterprises.

By drawing our attention to this important fact, the debunkers have made a major contribution to an understanding of the big-city public schools. Yet although the debunkers overturned one major misconception, they remained constrained by an even more basic point of view. While they quite properly shifted the focus of analysis from input to output, they persisted in framing their analyses solely in terms of the conventional beneficiaries of the schools, the school children.

23

The problem with such a perspective is that it is too narrow for properly assessing the productivity of the public schools. The schools provide benefits to others beside school children. No less than a profit-oriented enterprise, the schools may be viewed in terms of those who derive benefits in addition to the conventional consumers of the schools' product. Accordingly, a more useful approach involves casting the analysis of productivity in a framework which is broad enough to encompass what may be regarded as the basic set of beneficiaries of an organization. These beneficiaries are owner, management, labor, and the conventional beneficiary, usually clients.[4]

Owners basically benefit from the profits produced by an organization's activities. In the public sector, elected public officials may be regarded as the functional equivalents of owners, and, therefore, election to office is comparable to profits. Owners also may benefit by the acquisition of influence and power, as in the illustrative case of private-sector owners dominating the politics of a community by virtue of the wealth or large supply of jobs provided by their organization. Countless communities are constrained in their politics as a result of the overbearing presence of a local giant firm. What is deemed good for the giant becomes an imperative for the community.

Owners may profit, too, by the jobs produced by an enterprise. An organization may be used by its owners to take care of their own, so to speak. The time-honored instance of this type of ownership activity occurs in politics, going by the name of patronage. Regardless of the manifest intent of a given public enterprise, the politicians may regard its principal purpose as producing contractual and personnel patronage to be distributed among their followers.

The range of benefits acquired by management and labor generally is more restricted, consisting principally of the jobs produced by the organization. Nevertheless, the types of jobs acquired from a firm will range across a wide spectrum, and, therefore, jobs are crucial benefits, subject to considerable struggle and conflict. Traditionally, management has fallen on the plus side of the employment-benefits spectrum, and labor on the minus side, producing labor unions in between the two for the purpose of redressing the imbalance.

Management's success in modern times can be attributed largely to its ability to gain control over the authority structure of the organization, displacing the owners. The takeover has occurred in the public as well as the private sector, representing in the public sector what is referred to as a "reformed" form of government. It is not unusual under such an arrangement to find management augmenting its position within the organization, often at the expense of the other beneficiaries of the enterprise.

The conventional consumer benefits from whatever goods or services are produced by an organization. A classic point of view, liberalism, holds that autonomy is the significant factor determining the extent of benefits to be derived by the conventional consumer. When the consumer is dependent on a sole source or a rigged market, his consumption decisions are merely formal,

25

since no genuine choice is available. However, it is contended that once choice is provided, the consumer gains control over the market by dispensing and withholding his favor. He rewards those firms that best satisfy his needs and ultimately drives the worst firms out of the marketplace.

Advocates of this point of view increasingly have come to argue for importing liberal schemes into government. The ills of government stem largely from its monopoly position in the marketplace, say the advocates; accordingly, increased competition is the cure. Voucher systems for public school parents, direct cash grants for welfare recipients, and legislative funding for competing bureaucracies are some of the most popular versions of public-sector liberalism. The solution in all cases places a good deal of faith in the consumers' ability to take proper advantage of their new-found autonomy.[5]

Using the basic-set-of-beneficiaries framework for analyzing an organization's productivity can produce several useful distinctions concerning the value and direction of the organization's output, and it can direct attention to several relationships involved in the organization's productivity. The fundamental question brought into focus by the framework is which of an organization's beneficiaries benefits the most from the organization's activities. With regard to the particular public organization in which we are interested, the big-city schools, the guiding question of primary beneficiary enables us to substantially reinterpret the conventional understanding of the development and utility of the public schools.

The conventional interpretation of the development of the big-city public schools informed us as to the institutional elaboration of the enterprise, while only offering inferences as regards productivity. The debunking studies, on the other hand, while focusing on actual productivity, did so too narrowly. They informed us that the schools are an unsuccessful public enterprise. Addressing the broader question of which, if any, of the basic beneficiaries benefits from the schools may enable the determination of more fruitful conclusions. It may well be that the big-city public schools have been a highly successful organization from the point of view of their less conventional beneficiaries.

When much of the literature on urban politics and school politics is read from such a perspective, it is evident that such indeed is the case. All three of the unconventional beneficiaries of the public schools have been highly successful consumers of the schools' product. No less important, the basic-set-of-beneficiaries framework directs attention to the fact that at various stages different beneficiaries have been able to consume much more successfully than other beneficiaries of the schools. Finally, by examining these variable relationships more closely, a close correspondence can be identified between the type of beneficiary in a position of dominance and the prevailing form of big-city governance. Which is to say, while the conventional consumers, the school children, are the beneficiaries of the big-city schools product by right, so to speak, it invariably has been the unconventional beneficiaries who have possessed the might and the means of shaping the schools to serve primarily their interests instead.[6]

Traditionally, the big-city politicians have been the dominant beneficiary of the public schools. During the nineteenth century and early part of the twentieth century, the public schools formed an integral part of the patronage and spoils systems maintained by the boss and machine-rule politicians. Accordingly, the schools were structured in such a manner that they produced a wide and substantial variety of benefits for the politicians, namely patronage jobs and financial resources via contractual patronage.

During this period, the other beneficiaries of the schools, the school managers, teachers, and children, received only minor benefits from the schools. The wages from employment in the schools were low, job security at all levels of the school system was virtually nonexistent, and the decision-making authority that existed in the schools was confined to the trivial. The school children fared hardly any better, receiving mainly custodial care rather than academic instruction. Accordingly, the big-city public schools during the period of boss and machine rule may well be characterized as an owner-dominated organization, since earlier we noted that politicians most closely approximate the position of owners in the public sector.[7]

As reform rule displaced machine rule in the big cities, the managers of the public schools replaced the politicians as the dominant beneficiary of the schools. In establishing their dominant position, the school managers introduced a novel mechanism of hegemony into big-city politics: specialized academic credentials. Prior to the takeover, the academic training of the school managers generally had been indistinguishable from that of the teachers. Consequently, the managers had been unable to defend their management position in the schools on the basis of expert knowledge. However, with their certification as trained administrators, the managers gained the support of reform-oriented political leadership, who regarded functional expertise as the new badge of merit. The managers also received the support of the business elite, reform rule's principal backers, who were keen on extending their private-sector managerial revolution into government.

With their specialized administrative credentials in hand and the support of the reformers at hand, the school managers were able to alter the productivity of the big-city public schools in the three critical ways. Of foremost importance, from the new managers' viewpoint, school management positions were transformed from a limited number of politically dependent jobs into an increasingly large number of permanent careers. From this vantage point, the managers proceeded to restructure the schools into an increasingly elaborate hierarchical organization, through which the managers were then able to thoroughly dominate the teachers and the clientele of the schools. Finally, as the functional necessity of the management role in the schools became well established, the managers were able to greatly reduce external control over school affairs. The school board was largely reduced to selecting superintendents, parents were confined to ceremonial participation through involvement in structures such as the PTA, and the politicians were reduced to performing the ignominious task of raising revenue for the schools. Accordingly, in contradistinction to the preceding period of machine rule, under reform rule the public schools clearly had become management oriented and dominated.[8]

However, beginning in the early 1960s a new competitor began to rival the school managers for the position of dominant beneficiary of the schools. The new beneficiary is the school teachers. Once again, a novel mechanism was introduced by the insurgent group to establish dominance. The basis of machine rule had been the mechanisms of patronage and spoils, while reform rule was rooted in specialized academic training. The teachers used the union contract and the support of organized trade unions outside the schools to establish and advance their consumer interests.

Initially, the teachers used the union contract and their labor allies to restructure the public schools so that they began producing the traditional products of trade unionism: higher wages, increased job security, and improved working conditions. One union president succinctly stated his objectives along just such traditional lines, shortly after his teachers had acquired the right to collective bargaining. "Salaries are the first thing. I want to get the highest salaries in the country. Then, we can work on class size."[9]

Subsequently, however, a number of teachers' unions have set their sights on acquiring far greater benefits from the schools. The union contract is coming to be regarded as a mechanism for leveling the hierarchical structure of the school system. In its place the unions are advocating that the school authority structure come under the governance of the principle of codetermination, with the union leadership in conjunction with the formal management of the schools setting policy. Ultimately, the unions may be seeking an even grander role.

> The American Federation of Teachers is determined to control the public schools of the United States. And someday it will. Just as the American Medical Association controls American medicine and as the American Bar Association controls the legal profession."[10]

The transformation in urban rule corresponding to the teachers' achievement of consumer dominancy in the schools is less dramatic than the earlier shift from machine rule to reform rule. Essentially, the transformation involves a twofold decline. The big-city political party is experiencing a serious decline in organizational strength, and organized labor is experiencing a similar decline in its organizational strength.

The decline of the big-city political party is mainly attributable to a vastly reduced patronage base. The sharp decline of their patronage base necessitated a search by the leadership of the big-city political parties for an alternative source of organized political support. Not unexpectedly, given the interdependency, the politicians focused on the burgeoning governmental workforce as a potential major source of support. In their efforts to transform the potential base into an actual base of political support, the political leadership has had to make a series of substantial concessions to the governmental employees, including granting their demands for the right to collective bargaining.[11]

Much the same type of relationship has developed between big-city public employees and organized labor. In recent years the principal source of membership for organized labor has declined with the shift in the economy from a labor to a service base. At the same time, the governmental workforce, particularly at the state and local levels, has shown a rapid and large rate of increase. Consequently, organized labor has come to regard city public employees as a potential source of salvation in much the same manner as the leadership of the political party has. In order to bring the public employees into the fold, organized labor has had to devote a considerable amount of support to achieving the goals sought by the public employees. The outcome has been a greater or lesser degree of union rule in big cities across the country.[12]

In the remainder of this chapter, the historical relationships between the three primary beneficiaries of the schools and the three corresponding forms of urban government will be examined in greater detail. The relationships will be analyzed as they have occurred in one major city, Chicago, for reasons which were considered in the preceding chapter. The purpose of the detailed analysis is threefold. It will provide a partial test of the union-rule thesis that has been proposed. It also will provide a comprehensive and useful history of the development and political usage of a major public school system; and while Chicago's school politics will display differences in degree from other big-city school politics, they still ought to represent the generic kinds of changes experienced by all big-city school systems. Finally, the detailed examination provides a useful context for the extended analysis of union rule which follows in the remaining chapters.

Machine Rule's Beneficiary: The Politicians and the Schools

> The temper of the times accepted use of public office for private profit and personal power as a matter of course, and there were few open protests against it. Some school board members expressed surprised irritation at any criticism of the manipulation of school lands and contracts, or of appointments and promotions. As in other cities of the United States, [in Chicago] government employees were expected to show their "loyalty" and gratitude not by doing their work well, but by helping those who provided their jobs to remain in power. Teachers, who constituted approximately half the city employees, were included in this system as a matter of course. Those who failed to show the required "loyalty" could expect to be dismissed without further ado.[13]

So observes Mary Herrick in her useful history of Chicago's public schools. Herrick's description applies specifically to late nineteenth-century Chicago. However, it would apply nearly as well to much of the first half of twentieth-century Chicago, during the boss-rule reign of Mayor William Thompson (1915–1922 and 1927–1930), and during the machine-rule period under Mayor Edward Kelly (1933–1946). What Herrick's description makes abundantly clear is that this was a time when the public schools were dominated by the politicians through the patronage and spoils system. In turn, it is no less evident that the primary beneficiary of the schools under this arrangement was the politicians.

The politicians used the schools to assist them in securing their primary objective, political office. As it usually happens, political offices go to those with well-organized political campaigns. Being expensive and labor-intensive affairs, well-organized campaigns require plentiful amounts of money and manpower. Accordingly, the would-be politician requires financial resources to support his campaign and jobs to attract earnest campaign workers. Therein lies the great attraction of the public schools for the big-city politicians. The public schools historically have constituted an especially valuable source of both money and manpower for the politicians.

Compared to other big-city public bureaucracies, the schools provided jobs more abundant in number, more varied in kind, and more widely dispersed throughout the city. The school system always has been the city's largest public agency, both in terms of number of employees and expenditure. The schools also provide a wide range of employment. Within every school district in the city, janitors, nurses, clerks, social workers, engineers, truant officers, sundry bureaucrats, and a remarkable variety of maintenance specialists can be found working alongside an equally impressive array of instructional personnel: teachers, consultants, coordinators, supervisors, and educational and so-called support specialists of one sort or another. The especial political value of school jobs is therefore obvious: they can be distributed among every district and to virtually every socioeconomic and cultural/ethnic group in the city.

The schools similarly have represented an abundant and varied financial resource for the politicians. The schools regularly supply businessmen and tradesmen with a great array of heating, electrical, and other mechanical contracts; a variety of consultancies; numerous bricks and mortar projects; and a virtually inexhaustible flow of consumables purchases. Thus, come election time, the politicians are inclined to look to those who have benefited or can expect to benefit by their term in office for a campaign contribution. Anxious, grateful or simply prudent businessmen often will go along with the solicitation, and as investments go, a political contribution often makes more sense than, say, advertising does.

The public schools continued to be used mainly in this manner by the politicians until 1917, at which point an extraordinary break occurred in the political hold on the schools. The break was produced by the state legislature, which approved a genuinely radical package of reform legislation involving the Chicago schools. Interestingly, the pressure applied on the state legislators to approve the legislation was the unintended by-product of pressure which the Chicago politicians had been applying upon the schools to keep their control intact. Instead of continued control, however, the pressure produced a scandal, and of course scandals are the answered prayers of political "outs."

The "outs" in this instance were the leadership of the Chicago Teachers' Union. Virtually the entire union leadership had been dismissed by the school board, which for the occasion of the dismissal had created a ruling forbidding teacher affiliation with any labor organization. The dismissal served to foster an alliance between the teachers and organized labor, as well as a number of "good government" organizations that were outraged by the board's action. Consequently, the teachers were able to lobby the state legislators as a part of a broad-based coalition favoring progressive school reform, rather than merely as the victims of a local school board.[14]

The teachers and their allies managed to accomplish a number of legislative changes in the "rules of the game." These changes advantaged two of the beneficiaries in the basic set, the school managers and teachers, while they disadvantaged the politicians. The fourth beneficiary in the set, the school children, presumably was thought to be advantaged indirectly through the gains made by the teachers and managers.

School management benefited from the legislation in two significant ways. First, the school superintendent was provided with a four-year term of office, in place of annual reappointment by the school board. This enabled the superintendent to act and plan without the constrictive necessity of continually having to test the political winds. At the same time, it gave the superintendent more time and resources with which to build a political constituency of his own.

In addition to gaining some autonomy, the superintendent was given a significant measure of control over the teachers. He and two others of his choosing were to comprise a Board of Examiners. This change formally introduced the principle of merit promotion into the schools, and by leaving the determination of merit up to the superintendent and his appointees, the superintendent's control over the teachers was greatly enhanced. At the same time, of course, the informal system of political sponsorship, which had been governing promotions, suffered a severe setback.

The principal gain made by the teachers was the receipt of tenure. The legislation provided for indefinite tenure after a three-year probationary period. Specific procedures for teacher dismissal also were spelled out in the legislation. The tenure provision thus had the revolutionary effect of transforming what always had been patronage jobs into permanent teaching careers. For the first time, teachers were out from under the political dependency system. No more mandatory precinct work, peddling or if necessary "eating" tickets for political benefits, or bowing in general to the demands of a political sponsor—at least, that is, after the three-year probation period had been passed.

Getting the reforms enacted, however, as difficult as that had been, turned out to be a far more manageable task than implementing them. The basic purpose of the reforms was to separate the schools from city politics, and to thereby replace political control of the schools with school managerial control. However, the politicians hardly were willing to let go of a source of money and manpower as bountiful as the schools. Nor were the teachers enthusiastic supporters of a system of unilateral managerial control over the school policy-making process.

Given the gross disparities in power between the politicians and the teachers, it was the politicians who carried out the actions assuring that Chicago's schools would remain for a longer while unreformed. Yet, the teachers served as willing accomplices in partially undoing the reform of the schools. While the politicians were doing their utmost to reassert external political control over the schools, the teachers raised very little protest whatsoever.

The showdown between the reformers and the politicians and teachers came early. Shortly after the governor signed the reforms into law, the Chicago school board, led by a former close ally of Mayor Thompson turned renegade, enlisted a group of prominent citizens to find a new superintendent of schools. The prominent citizens lost no time in coming up with a candidate from outside the city who had solid reform credentials, Charles Chadsey, superintendent of the Detroit schools. The school board approved the search committee's choice, and then compounded its audacity by hiring Chadsey without consulting Mayor Thompson.

Thompson responded in kind by turning Chadsey into a campaign issue, vowing to "kick Chadsey out" if reelected. Upon winning a second term, Thompson appointed a new school board, which immediately set about fulfilling Thompson's campaign pledge. After completing less than one year of his legislatively mandated four-year term, Superintendent Chadsey resigned following extensive harassment by the school board.

The board then signed on a more conventionally oriented superintendent, Peter Mortenson. Mortenson had excellent political credentials, since he had aided the school board in its harassment and ouster of Chadsey. Mortenson carried the same politically sensitive, cooperative attitude with him into the superintendency. Thus, the politicians experienced little resistance in reasserting their control over the schools, and in spite of the legislature's landmark school reforms, it was mainly business as usual in the Chicago schools.

The teachers' sharply divergent attitude toward Superintendents Chadsey and Mortenson is instructive in pointing to the primary interests of the teachers. The reformer Chadsey received no support from the teachers while he was being harassed by the politicians. Instead the teachers, as well as the school principals, criticized Chadsey for failing to heed their advice on a number of school issues. The teachers also expressed suspicions about Chadsey because his main supporter was a school board member who earlier had directed the dismissal of the teacher union leadership because of the union's labor affiliation.

On the other hand, the teachers proved to be one of Mortenson's few supporters—besides, of course, the politicians who were benefiting from Mortenson's compliant administration. The courts had publicly criticized Mortenson for his participation in the harassment of Chadsey, and the media and the reform movement castigated him for enabling the politicians to renew their plundering of the schools. Yet, the teachers expressed nothing but high regard for Mortenson's administration. In 1923 when Mortenson submitted his resignation, the teachers went on record:

> . . . to express their appreciation of the services rendered to the children of Chicago and to the cause of education by Superintendent Peter A. Mortenson, who, through the Class Room Teachers' Councils, is utilizing for the benefit of the school system, the collective experience of the classroom teachers, gained by daily personal contact with the children.[15]

Mortenson also provided the teachers with the largest salary increase they had received in half a century. Thus, they were willing to overlook the superintendent's subservience to the politicians because he had looked after teacher interests so effectively. While the benefits themselves undoubtedly were a basis for the teachers' high regard, of value, too, was that conferral of the benefits constituted a clear recognition by Mortenson that the teachers were a legitimate beneficiary of the schools.

Notwithstanding the teachers' assessment of the Mortenson superintendency, by 1923 school affairs had gotten decidedly out of hand. Mayor Thompson's chief advisor was indicted for directing twenty-three coconspirators, including several school board members, in a $1 million plundering of the school treasury and for engaging in kickback schemes with school contractors. Thompson's man managed to slip by with a remarkable acquittal. However, the scandal sank Thompson. He reluctantly announced that he would not be a candidate for reelection in the upcoming 1923 mayoralty. The schools scandal also paved the way for an even more remarkable occurrence: the election of Chicago's first reform mayor.

Reform Rule's Beneficiary: The
Administrators and the Schools

Reform rule arrived late in Chicago and it left early. The city's first reform mayor, William Dever, was not elected until 1924, and he was defeated after a single term in office. The political machine then held City Hall for nearly the next twenty years. In 1946 the machine ran into another major scandal, involving again, significantly enough, the schools. The machine coped with this scandal by employing a clever camouflage: it slated its own reform candidate.

This produced Chicago's second and, as it turned out, final reform mayor, Martin Kennelly. The machine allowed its reform mayor to serve two terms. Then it reemerged fully intact, dumped Kennelly, and slated a candidate of more moderate persuasion, Richard Daley, who served the city for the next twenty-one years. On the eve of Daley's victory, one of Chicago's redoubtable ward committeemen declared, "Chicago ain't ready for reform," and he certainly had the weight of evidence on his side.

Nevertheless, Chicago's two brief flings with reform rule did leave a telling and lasting effect upon the relationship between the schools and the politicians and upon the manner in which the schools are managed. The extent to which a big-city public agency may be said to be reformed can be assessed by the following three criteria: the extent to which its operation is insulated from the city's politics, the extent to which it operates as a bureaucracy, and the extent of the professionalization of its personnel.[16] By these criteria, as we shall see, Chicago's public schools are well reformed. Moreover, the schools are one of the city's few reformed public agencies. Thus, reform rule has had a unique impact on the city's schools. How this came to pass in the last of the great machine cities is the subject of this section.[17]

In 1924 the newly appointed school board of reform mayor William Dever brought in a new school superintendent, William McAndrew, whose arrival had the aspects of a triumphant homecoming. Years earlier, McAndrew had served as a high school principal in Chicago; while doing so he stood by a teacher's daring decision to demote a politician's child and, as it turned out, the decision cost McAndrew his job. However, he went on to eventually become a superintendent of schools in Brooklyn, and over the years gained a reputation as one of the nation's leading reform educators. Thus, McAndrew's return to Chicago's schools symbolized the triumph of professionalism over political domination, and the teachers were enthralled. Margaret Haley, the nationally renowned leader of the Chicago teachers' organization and an ardent foe of political interference in the schools, declared McAndrew to be no less than one of the three foremost educators in the country.

However, disenchantment set in almost immediately. For it quickly became clear from McAndrew's reform agenda that he regarded teachers who desired a role in the decision-making process as hardly any less an enemy of reform than the plundering politicians. The politicians obviously had to be driven from the schools; otherwise the schools could not be administered on a professional basis. No less importantly, the teachers had to be put in their proper place too, which turned out to be at the bottom of a rigidly hierarchical bureaucracy. After all, the schools had to be administered on a modern, efficient basis, which of course entailed a clearly demarcated and monocratic chain of command. Thus, with the teachers down and the politicians out, the administrators were left alone and on top to provide unilateral and expert direction of school affairs.

What reform rule accomplished, then, in terms of the basic-set-of-beneficiaries framework was the creation of an additional dimension in the time-
honored struggle over the schools' product between the politicians and· the
schoolmen. Out of the relatively homogeneous schoolmen grouping, reform rule
forged a distinct subset, school administrators. Reform rule aided the administrators in establishing and advancing their particular interests over and against
the interests of the teachers by giving the administrators a free hand in directing
the schools. Not once during reform Mayor Dever's term of office did he intervene in school affairs, although the problems created by the school administrators
clearly were numerous and serious enough to adversely affect Dever's reelection
prospects.

The problem in general with providing administrators with a free hand is the
increased likelihood that the administrators will structure an organization to
serve principally their own interests—or, at least, they will not take other interests into sufficient regard in formulating policy. Which is to say, administrators
will behave much as any other group when provided with the opportunity to
operate in an unchecked manner. In turn, the other beneficiaries in the basic
set can be expected to create a great deal of discord, inasmuch as the changes
introduced by reform rule leave them in a highly disadvantageous position from
which to contend for their benefits.

So it was, that during Superintendent McAndrew's reform administration
the city's schools were full of turbulence. The new beneficiaries, the school
administrators, sought to establish their dominance, and in doing so they pat-
terned their behavior after and closely allied themselves with reform rule's
principal backers, the businessmen. This meant that the watchword of the new
school administration was efficiency, and any group that impeded the administrators' conception of how greater efficiency could be attained was necessarily
in jeopardy. Thus, on the one hand, all three of McAndrew's major reforms were
in keeping with the practices and objectives of the nation's leading progressive
educators. On the other hand, each reform can be seen to have had a highly
adverse effect on the politicians and the teachers. Part of the conflict was
philosophical, but much of it was practical.

McAndrew's foremost reform, in that it paved the way for implementing
the other two, was the curtailment of political and teacher influence on school
policy making. In his first annual report, Superintendent McAndrew offered
evidence as to his accomplishments in the elimination of political influence upon
his behavior. During the first year, 520 attempts had been made to influence
him; however, by the second year, the efforts were reduced to a mere five.

McAndrew promptly terminated teacher influence also. The Teacher Coun-
cils, which had flourished under his predecessor Mortenson's administration, were
abolished. When the school board advised the superintendent that the council
had been mandated by a board ruling, McAndrew proceeded to create a new
form of council which included principals, other managers, and even truant

officers in addition to teachers. The change effectively left the teachers without sufficient voting strength to carry any issue.

Streamlining the policy-making process along strictly nonpolitical and hierarchical lines enabled McAndrew to readily alter the teachers' working conditions. He introduced efficiency ratings, increased the workload, cut back on school holidays, installed time sheets that required four sign-ins per day, and set highly unrealistic performance standards. The reforms were accompanied by public criticisms from Superintendent McAndrew of the teachers' efficiency levels and efforts, both of which he declared to be far below acceptable professional standards.

The most controversial means that McAndrew used to increase the teachers' workload was the introduction of the so-called Gary Plan. The plan basically involved platooning students between instructional programs and enrichment/supervised play activities. This accommodated a substantially larger number of students within the same space confines, and at the same time the students received a longer school day and a much broader curriculum. The program thus represented a happy marriage of the ideals of progressive educators and the cost consciousness of the business community.

However, from the teachers' point of view the program simply amounted to an additional burdening of what they regarded as an already overworked teaching staff. Organized labor also strongly opposed the program. As an interest group in the schools, labor was an advocate of increased expenditures, and they perceived the Gary Plan as a program backed by business interests to obviate the need for greater expenditures to reduce class size. The fact that the program originated in Gary, Indiana, the company town of strongly anti-union U.S. Steel, made the program's opposition virtually a labor crusade. Finally, given the clear-cut social class conflict that was involved, politicians interested in ousting the reformers from City Hall were provided a classically proportioned issue around which to launch a campaign.[18]

McAndrew's third major school reform went, albeit indirectly, right to the heart of organized teacher interests. The superintendent replaced the prevailing 8-4 form of grade structure with a junior high school component. While the change was again in a direction favored by progressive educators, the reform posed a number of critical problems for the largest and most influential teacher organization, the Chicago Teachers' Federation.

The main problem was that the federation was housed primarily in the elementary grades. Thus, by creating a junior high school which included the seventh and eighth grades, the federation's primary source of membership was reduced by 25 percent. To make matters worse, McAndrew instituted a special qualifying examination for the junior high school teaching positions. The problem here was that the federation's core consisted largely of older teachers with less formal training than the younger teachers in the system; thus, the federation's main supporters were left at a competitive disadvantage on the qualifying exam. Both problems meant that the federation virtually was compelled to oppose the junior highs, and this led to the federation's third big problem. By opposing the junior high schools, the federation was bound to antagonize the junior high teachers and thereby assure that few of them would support the federation in the future.

As a result of McAndrew's harsh reign of reform, an unprecedented number of teachers, led by Margaret Haley of the Chicago Teachers' Federation, switched their allegiance from reform to machine rule by supporting Big Bill Thompson's bid for mayor against Dever in 1927. Organized labor also endorsed the Thompson candidacy, in part because McAndrew's school reforms were interpreted as an element of Mayor Dever's commitment to "big business." Thompson adroitly exploited the disaffection of the teachers and labor by fervently pledging if elected to "boot McAndrew back to Wall Street." As it turned out, Thompson was successful, gaining 54 percent of the vote.

What a difference the 4 percent made. With the downfall of Dever came nearly twenty uninterrupted years of machine rule. One of Thompson's first acts upon regaining the mayor's office was to show his ingratitude to the teachers for their campaign support. He fired hundreds of teachers serving in school clerical jobs, and replaced them with temporary civil service employees. "Temps," as they are called, are not required to pass a civil service exam, and when the Civil Service Commission is politically dominated, as it was then and still is today, a temp serves indefinitely at the pleasure of a political sponsor.

Two comparisons more generally show the use that Thompson and his Democratic successors, Anton Cermak and Edward Kelly, made of the public schools. Table 2-1 indicates that with respect to other local jurisdictions, the public schools began receiving a substantially smaller share of tax revenues. Moreover, the distribution falls neatly along a dimension of patronage employment: the greater the level of patronage, the greater the share of revenue received.

Table 2-1
Property Tax Rates: Chicago Metropolitan Area, 1931-1932

Government Branch	1931 Rate	1932 Rate	Percentage Change
Sanitary District	0.56	0.87	+55%
Park District	0.79	0.99	+25%
County Board	0.52	0.58	+13%
City	2.52	2.82	+12%
Board of Education	2.46	2.03	−21%

Source: Cook County Treasurer, State of Illinois. Cited in Mary Herrick, *The Chicago Schools: A Social and Political History* (Beverly Hills, Cal.: Sage Publications, 1971), p. 219. Reprinted with permission.

Both the Sanitary and Park Districts relied exclusively upon a system of patronage employment. The County Board and the City, on the other hand, employed a mixed civil-service and patronage system, with the greater bulk of jobs coming under the patronage system. Thus, the schools, with their large contingent of tenured teachers, represented the most politically independent branch of local government, and they were treated accordingly by the political machine's leadership.

A second comparison serves to corroborate the patronage-based distribution principle. Within the school system, virtually all of the noninstructional jobs were distributed on a patronage basis. Teaching jobs, on the other hand, were covered under the 1917 tenure law. Thus, the instructional branch of the school system was far more politically independent, and once again resources followed patronage.

A U.S. Office of Education survey conducted during 1936 similarly showed that of the nation's ten largest cities Chicago's schools ranked highest in noninstructional costs and lowest in instructional costs. Table 2-2 furthermore indicates the extent to which Chicago's allocation of administrative costs differed from that of two comparable big cities. Thus, the machine clearly made use of the schools to suit its own interests. Areas of the schools from which the politicians benefited were rewarded with greater revenues; areas not serving as effectively were penalized.

Chicago's second fling with reform rule came in 1946, once again amidst a major schools scandal. The North Central Association, a school accreditation agency, had been warning the Chicago schools since 1933 of serious deficiencies and threatening loss of accreditation. However, because of the machine's considerable influence, the reports never were made public nor was any action taken. Finally, however, the press secured a copy of North Central's damaging assessment in 1946, and the matter then was transformed from a minor annoyance into a major disaster.

Faced with several other scandals and serious problems as well, and after a number of unsuccessful attempts to mollify the critics, the machine's leadership came up with an extraordinary solution. The machine dumped Mayor Kelly

Table 2-2
Administrative Cost Distribution: Three Major Cities in 1936

Category	Chicago	New York	Philadelphia
Business administration	82.9%	34.5%	29.7%
Education administration	17.1%	65.5%	70.3%

Source: William Reavis, 1936. Cited in Mary Herrick, *The Chicago Schools: A Social and Political History* (Beverly Hills, Cal.: Sage Publications, 1971), p. 228. Reprinted with permission.

and slated its own reform candidate, a widely respected businessman, Martin Kennelly. The strategy proved to be successful, and, as Kennelly was in many respects a genuine reformer, he promptly turned over the schools to a nationally renowned, reform-oriented superintendent, Herold Hunt.

Hunt was definitely no McAndrew, proving that even before he arrived. He refused to accept the superintendency unless it was expanded to include jurisdiction over the entire school system, rather than merely the instructional branch. Under normal circumstances, Hunt may as well have asked for the moon. The noninstructional branch of the schools was part of the politicians' patronage system, and it had remained so because the politicians rather than the school administrators controlled access to the jobs. Yet, with the accreditation scandal hanging heavily over the schools, circumstances were decidedly abnormal and the politicians reluctantly accepted Hunt's outrageous terms.

The worst of the politicians' misgivings quickly proved to be well founded. Hunt established an autonomous department of personnel, required all school employees to pass examinations in order to acquire jobs, and within two years school patronage was virtually abolished. Thus, for the first time in Chicago's history, the school system was operating in its entirety independently of the city's political system.[19]

The significance of Hunt's reforms merits emphasis. Abolishing school personnel patronage eliminated the major incentive for the politicians' regular intervention in school affairs. Whereas McAndrew had constructed barriers around the school system which prevented the politicians from intervening, Hunt, by doing away with the basis for intervention, found there was no need to fend off the politicians. The politicians no longer showed much interest in the schools. Thus, in terms of our basic-set-of-beneficiaries framework, Hunt's reform reduced the long-standing three-way contest over the schools' product to mainly a two-way struggle between the school administrators and the teachers. Moreover, as long as the managers retained unilateral control over the school decision-making processes, the contest was very likely to remain one-sided.

Hunt's successor, Benjamin Willis, demonstrated just how managerially dominant a reformed school system could in fact become. Willis sought to carry the logic of reform to its ultimate conclusion: the elimination of all lay influence on school affairs. He came closer to succeeding than any other school superintendent ever has. Parental, political, school board, and teacher influence were curtailed severely during the years of the Willis administration.

Parental involvement of any significant sort was actively discouraged by Willis. School telephone numbers were not even listed in the public phone directories. The president of the Chicago Region PTA was kept waiting two years for a meeting with the superintendent. As many a reformer will, Willis was fond of drawing a parallel between educational relationships and the coveted doctor–patient relationship. "I know of no patient who, upon entering a hospital, dictates to the physician concerning the program of medication. His family does not do so either."[20] So it was to be with the city's schools, as long as Willis had his way.

The school board fared hardly any better in Willis's scheme of things. In spite of the board's mandate to formulate policy for the schools, Willis regarded the board as falling essentially within the same lay category as pupils, parents, and politicians. He therefore excluded the school board from the divine circle whenever he could, and over the years Willis's domination of the board became virtually absolute. The extent of his domination can be seen from a quintessential reform agreement which he managed to extract from the school board. The agreement had two principal terms. Board members were to turn over all correspondence which they received concerning school affairs to the superintendent; in that way Willis could be kept informed as to the extent of the board's knowledge about the schools. Board members also were required to limit their contact with the schools exclusively to the superintendent. Thus, Willis had the board coming and going.[21]

The teachers and the politicians had it somewhat better with Willis, but, to be sure, both were kept in their proper place—far from the school decision-making structure. Willis placated both sources of traditional opposition mainly with money, and he did it in a manner which did not antagonize the business community, with which he was on highly favorable terms. The teachers received an unprecedented series of salary increases, which Willis insisted were long overdue given the teachers' professional status. On the other hand, Willis steadfastly refused to grant the teachers collective-bargaining rights, which he said was not an appropriate means by which professionals ought to conduct their affairs.

In much the same manner, the politicians were kept more or less content. Willis launched an unprecedented school building program, which earned him the nickname "Ben the Builder." There was never a hint of scandal associated with the project and the buildings were constructed for very reasonable amounts of money, factors which brought Willis praise from the business community. On the other hand, the building project was so huge that the politicians were bound to profit from the donations of the grateful businessmen engaged in the city's unprecedented building effort.

It ultimately took an intense, widely supported, and protracted civil rights revolt to topple the well-fortified Willis reform fortress. When it eventually became clear to the politicians and the businessmen that Willis would persist in treating the demands of the civil rights groups just as cavalierly as he did the requests of parent, teachers, and school board members, Willis finally lost their support.[22] The school board accepted Willis's resignation in 1966.

At the time, it appeared to many observers that the black parents and civil rights groups allied with them would become regular and powerful actors in the city's school politics. This of course would have added still another dimension to the struggle over the schools' product, and conceivably it would have finally given the conventional consumer a significant role in school affairs. However, it was the teachers rather than the blacks who wound up adding the new dimension to school politics. In the same year that Willis's resignation was accepted by the school board, the board also granted collective-bargaining rights to the teachers. The grant marked the beginning of the end of the managerial dominance which reform rule so effectively had served to establish in the public schools.

Union Rule's Beneficiary: The Teachers and the Schools

According to a long-time, highly successful ward committeeman of the machine, the Chicago political organization depends for its success upon strict adherence to two cardinal principles: "Don't make no waves; don't back no losers."[23] The piety which the machine displays toward these two principles makes considerable practical sense. Backing losers fosters an impression of fallibility; such an impression serves to weaken the machine's hold upon the faithful, and it strengthens the resolve of the opposition at the same time. Waves are even worse. Waves create general instability, and particular waves can be transformed into effective campaign issues that an opposition can use to sweep the machine from office.

Not surprisingly, then, the machine's adherence to its principles has been strict enough. The machine has been swept from the mayor's office only twice, and, lending credence to the "Don't make waves" principle, on both occasions school scandals figured prominently in the sweep. The indictment of Mayor Thompson's chief advisor for plundering the school treasury swept Thompson from office, and the school accreditation scandal sank Mayor Kelly. Superintendent Willis's obdurate opposition to the civil righters created a third major wave. While the Willis wave did not drive the machine from the mayor's office, it did serve to radically alter the city's school politics.

Willis's departure was supposed to still the waters and provide the machine with an opportunity to put its constituency back together. However, no sooner had Willis announced his resignation than the teachers' union announced its intention to strike unless the school board granted the teachers collective-bargaining rights. Down with one wave and up comes another. The timing of the union's threat provided the teachers with leverage they never before had possessed. With the city still in a highly fragmented, volatile state, there was no telling what political implications were entailed by a teachers' strike.

The outcome was that the teachers' union got its way without even having to strike. The school board reversed its longstanding, adamant opposition and granted the teachers collective-bargaining rights by a solid vote of 7–2.[24] Thus, for the first time in Chicago's history, the teachers possessed a genuine, rather than only an advisory, role in the school policy-making structure. The stage, therefore, finally was set for the acquisition of benefits by the teachers at a rate and in a manner which was unprecedented.

Yet, the acquisition of collective-bargaining rights did not immediately produce a fully developed form of union rule. Collective bargaining is the basis for establishing union rule. However, the extent to which union rule actually develops depends upon the degree to which a union's leadership pursues an independently determined and narrowly self-interested course of action. Accordingly, during the early years of collective bargaining, from 1967 to 1972, the teacher union leadership developed what may be described as a moderate form of union rule. While the teachers acquired greater benefits than ever before, the union leadership's actions were formed in collaboration with the politicians, and the union leadership took into account the interests of the politicians as well as those of the teachers in determining an acceptable level of benefits.

By contrast, after 1972 the union leadership displayed a much more independently determined and self-interested form of behavior. The change in behavior was mainly the result of a change in the union's leadership. For it had become increasingly apparent over the years that as long as the union's leadership continued to defer to the interests of the politicians, teacher benefits would be acquired at a less than maximum rate. Thus, in the union's 1972 elections, the radicals were able to oust the moderate leadership from office.

Despite the radical orientation of the union's new leadership, it is important to recognize that the leadership frequently continued to rely upon the politicians for the acquisition of benefits. The two critical differences between the moderate and the militant leadership are that the new leadership is no longer willing to moderate its demands in deference to the interests of the politicians. In turn, when the politicians display a disinclination to participate in the settlement process, the new leadership will attempt to force political participation through a teacher strike.

Thus, collaboration between the union leadership and the politicians persists, but now the union leadership sets the terms. The progression, then, is from a moderate to a more fully developed form of union rule. This progression can better be understood by briefly examining the successive collective-bargaining negotiations which have taken place between the union and the school board from 1966 to 1978.

What is particularly revealing about the moderate behavior of the early teacher union leadership's behavior is that it points to the primary basis for the politicians' grant of collective-bargaining rights to the teachers. Instead of capitulating to the teachers' strike threat, the politicians seized upon the opportunity presented by the strike threat to regain a significant role in the school decision-making structure, a role they had not held since the schools had been reformed in 1946. Which is to say, the leadership of the teachers' union did not achieve the right to collective bargaining; rather, they had the right thrust upon them by the politicians. The politicians intended to use collective bargaining for their own as well as the teachers' benefit.

During every phase of the threatened teachers' strike to acquire the right to collective bargaining, the teacher union leadership actively opposed the strike.[25] Prior to the strike vote by the union's delegate body, the leadership renewed its long-standing commitment to the school board that the teachers would never strike the schools. Moreover, the leadership made its pledge while fully aware that the settlement to which it had agreed was far from acceptable to a number of the union's delegates. Therefore, in making the commitment the leadership clearly was endangering its leadership position within the union, and the delegates' meeting was bound at best to be a highly risky affair. As it turned out, the meeting was a disaster for the leadership. The settlement proposed by the leadership was rejected by a vote of 90–80. Even worse, the leadership was directed to secure not only better benefits but collective-bargaining rights as well. Otherwise, the teachers would strike, and a strike deadline was set for two weeks hence.[26]

Despite the severe setback, the union leadership persisted in honoring its commitment to the school board. The vote by the delegates was characterized by the union president as the unrepresentative act of a small group of radicals. According to the president, the radicals had packed the delegates' meeting and proceeded to intimidate a number of delegates who otherwise would have supported the leadership's position. More importantly, the union president also announced that he had received petitions from teachers urging that the delegates' vote be put to a referendum of the entire union membership.

Thus, the leadership seemed bent on overturning the delegates' action, and in all likelihood they possessed sufficient resources to succeed. The popularity of the union leadership was considerable. The president had been the union's principal founder and its first president, elected in 1937. His current term as president dated back two decades. The vice-president had held that office for ten years, and earlier he had been the union treasurer for five years.[27] The leadership also fully controlled the union newspaper, which was distributed to all union members. The combination of popularity and propaganda, then, probably would have been enough to overcome the radicals' slim margin of victory in the delegate body vote.

However, the issue never came to another vote. While the union leadership was pondering its predicament, the decision was being taken out of the leadership's hands by organized labor and the politicians. Five days after the delegates had voted narrowly to strike, the executive council of the Chicago Federation of Labor was voting unanimously to support the teachers' demand for collective bargaining. Additionally, the president of the CFL, William Lee, was interceding personally with Mayor Daley on the teachers' behalf, and Lee was a close, long-term advisor of the mayor.[28]

Organized labor's interest in the teachers represented a dramatic departure from a policy of indifference and even at times hostility which had existed since at least the Great Depression. The widespread unemployment produced by the Depression had driven organized labor into a close and subordinate relationship with the political machine. The basis for the unusual display of interest by labor in the teachers stemmed from the shift to a service base and the growth of the governmental labor force in the economy. Both of these developments made organized labor's traditional blue-collar, nongovernmental base of recruitment outdated and productive of stagnation. Even more pointedly instructive to organized labor was Walter Reuther's dramatic demonstration in New York City that with labor money, manpower, and know-how, even a miniscule and ineffectual teachers' organization such as the one headed by David Selden and Albert Shanker could be transformed into a sole collective-bargaining agent.[29] Then, with the Irish-Catholic President Kennedy's bestowal of bargaining rights upon federal employees, every respectable local labor leader must have felt the need for a public employee union or two within his fold.

At any rate, the mayor obviously had several reasons for respecting Bill Lee's support of the teachers. Nevertheless, organized labor in Chicago clearly is the "tail of the dog," and there were any number of reasons the mayor could have given organized labor for refusing to support granting the teachers collective bargaining. Not the least of the reasons was the precedent such a move would set for police, fire, and other city employees to demand a contract. Unlike the teachers, virtually all of the city's employees were still within the politicians' patronage domain, and thus collective bargaining for them had to be resisted at all costs. Yet, Daley did wind up giving approval to his allies on the school board to grant bargaining rights to the teachers.[30] Inasmuch as the strike could have been put down by the union leadership and labor's urging could have been reasonably resisted, the mayor must have discerned some compelling political benefits that would accrue from making the extraordinary grant to the teachers.

As it turned out, significant benefits were provided to the politicians as well as the teachers during the early, moderate years of union rule. However, the flaw inherent in the politicians' strategy turned up early also. For the acquisition of benefits by the politicians required the acquiescence of the union leadership to the politicians' interests. Yet, by serving the politicians' interests as well as the teachers', the union leadership in turn weakened its position within the union. In order for the politicians' strategy to succeed, then, the union leadership had to exercise a considerable degree of political skill, and, as it happened, the skills of the leadership were not up to the task.[31]

The pattern which governed collective-bargaining negotiations between the teachers' union and the school board during the years 1967–1972, the period of moderate union rule, can be described by two propositions. If the politicians participate in the settlement process as a mediator, then the teachers acquire a high level of benefits. If, however, the politicians do not choose to participate in the settlement process, then the teacher union leadership will not apply pressure to encourage the politicians' participation. Accordingly, the propositions entail two outcomes. The level of teacher benefits is determined primarily by the politicians. In turn, allowing the politicians to make the determination produces a lower level of teacher benefits. The interests of the politicians and the teachers simply are not parallel.

The flaw which was inherent in the politicians' strategy did not appear in the first two contract settlements. Both the politicians and the teachers reaped unprecedented benefits from the settlements as a result of Mayor Daley's mediation. The teachers' principal gain was increased income. Both contracts contained substantial salary increases, while the first also included a paid Christmas vacation and the second a paid spring vacation. Additionally, an elaborate formal grievance procedure was instituted, and nearly 1,000 substitute teachers were hired to reduce the workload of the regularly employed teachers.[32]

The principal gain made by the politicians was that for the first time an alliance was established between the teachers and the politicians. The teachers were the city's largest set of public employees and essentially the only public-employee group over whom the politicians had been able to exert little influence. Moreover, the teachers traditionally had been strongly reform oriented and therefore politically hostile to the machine. Collective bargaining altered all of these factors. It provided the teachers with a mechanism by which they could change the schools so that they began serving the teachers' interests. By participating in the settlement process as a mediator, the mayor received credit for being the instrumental distributor of teacher benefits. In effect, collective bargaining took the place of patronage as a means of securing the teachers' dependence on the machine.[33]

Sustaining such a relationship is, of course, no simple matter for the politicians. They must possess the capability of generating sufficient resources to finance the benefit increases provided to the teachers. Indeed, the mayor confronted the problem of limited resources after mediating only the second contract. The mayor had assumed the responsibility of underwriting the increases included in the first two agreements; however, he was only partially successful in acquiring the additional funds needed to finance the second settlement. Accordingly, the school board was faced with its first deficit as contract talks began in 1969. Because of this deficit, the board therefore advised the teachers' union that no salary increase could be provided that year.

The school board's decision left the union leadership in a difficult position. Once again the leadership would have to rely upon the politicians' support in order to acquire an increase in benefits. Unfortunately, this time the politicians declined to participate in the settlement process. The union leadership, therefore, had to decide whose interests it would serve: the politicians or the teachers. By declining to mediate, the politicians were indicating their preference for a settlement without an increase in teacher benefits. The teachers, on the other hand, obviously preferred an increase. In view of the impasse that had been reached, the concrete decision the union leadership had to make was whether or not to call for a strike.

The leadership decided against a strike by accepting the school board's offer of a contract with no increase in benefits. However, as soon as the leadership made its decision, the flaw in the politicians' strategy came promptly to light. The union membership rejected the leadership's settlement. However, rather than allowing a strike to be called, the leadership met and revised the terms of the settlement. It was changed from a one-year to a six-month agreement, after which point the leadership would then renegotiate for a salary increase with the school board. The change served to give the school board time to receive its appropriation from the legislature. Thus, the renegotiation would take place on a basis of actual rather than anticipated revenue.[34] The change indicates, then, that the leadership remained committed to its original position: to limit its demands to what the school board could finance or the politicians would pledge to finance.

The union's executive committee approved the revision by a vote of 21-10, and the membership endorsed the contingent settlement 9,662-5,206. Yet, while the leadership got out of the hole it had dug for itself, the votes clearly revealed that significant proportions of both the membership and the leadership would have preferred the union to adopt a more militant strategy instead of simply buying more time for a moderate set of objectives.[35]

When negotiations resumed in May of 1969, the leadership further confirmed its commitment to a moderate course of action. Against the objections of the leadership, the union embarked on two radical actions. First, it conducted a mass demonstration before the state legislature to demand greater funding for the schools; then the union struck the schools while the mayor was in the process of mediating a settlement. Yet in spite of the leadership's objections, the strike clearly produced a prompt and substantial gain for the teachers. After the strike had run just one day, Mayor Daley mediated a settlement which included a salary increase of 13 percent as well as several other benefits.[36] Once again the mayor also accepted responsibility for securing the additional funds needed to finance the generous agreement.

The settlement was approved overwhelmingly by the union's membership, 9,776-585. Indeed, there was only one dissenting voice raised to the terms of the settlement; however, as later events confirmed, it was a significant voice. Certain members of the union's negotiating team complained that the union president had been overly anxious to reach a settlement in order to end the strike. As a result, the settlement that was reached was less than what could have been secured through a longer strike.[37] Thus, even in moments of triumph, the union president's detractors could point to his limited efforts in pursuing the teachers' interests.

In the following year's negotiations, the union president supplied his union opponents with still more ammunition. He agreed to another settlement with no salary increase, and he did it in a manner which was bound to increase his image as an ineffectual negotiator. The president began by demanding a salary increase of 10 percent; after a few negotiating sessions, the demand was reduced to 6 percent; finally the demand for a raise was withdrawn.[38] The president also accepted the modest settlement one day prior to a scheduled strike vote. Thus, the president could readily be perceived as seeking to avoid a strike, even though it had just been demonstrated that a strike was highly productive in terms of increasing teacher benefits.

In any event, the membership approved the 1970 settlement by a wide margin. The leadership had managed to extract one significant benefit from the board. The length of service required to attain maximum salary was reduced substantially, which meant that the most senior teachers in the school system did receive a salary increase. This gain plus the fact that the teachers only recently had received their 1969 salary increase because of the late renegotiation session probably accounted for the teachers' support for the settlement.

In the 1971 negotiations, the general pattern which had governed the contract settlements broke down. Revealing once again the flaw inherent in the politicians' strategy, the break in the pattern was initiated by the militantly inclined delegate body of the union. While the delegates always had been consistent voters for striking in order to secure increased benefits, in 1971 their zeal reached new heights. They voted unanimously, 385-0, to strike unless the leadership secured a substantial settlement. The unanimity left the leadership with no basis whatsoever for pursuing a moderate course of action. Adding to the leadership's difficulties, the prospects for satisfying the delegates' demands seemed decidedly bleak. The school board insisted it had to hold the line, and the politicians once again were displaying no interest in intervening in the settlement process.

Impaled between the horns of its two now decidedly antagonistic interests, the leadership had little choice but to allow the negotiation process to lapse into a strike. Yet, the strike produced what the militantly inclined unionists had been insisting all along such an action would produce: political intervention and a substantial settlement as a result of the intervention. After the strike had run two days, the mayor stepped in to mediate, and the mediation in turn produced a novel two-year contract that included back-to-back salary increases of 8 percent.

However, the strike also produced just what the moderate leadership had been insisting it would: the dissatisfaction of the politicians with the union's militant behavior. Thus, after the militant delegates' vote had created the first break in the negotiation pattern by forcing the participation of the politicians in the settlement process, the politicians proceeded to produce a second significant break of their own. After mediating his usual generous settlement, the mayor declined to assume his usual responsibility of securing the funds needed to finance the settlement.

The immediate consequence of the mayor's decision was that the school board was left in the extraordinary position of having agreed to a settlement which it had virtually no possibility of financing. However, when possibilities run out, there are always lawyers. Facing an estimated deficit of $100 million, the school board declared in 1972 that a loophole existed in the contract which made fulfillment of the second year of the agreement contingent upon the availability of funds.[39] Accordingly, rather than an 8 percent salary increase, the teachers would receive no increase. The board furthermore announced that drastic measures would have to be taken in order to reduce the deficit. The schools would be closed early, entailing an additional loss of teacher income, and more than 4,500 positions would be eliminated from the budget. To make matters worse for the union leadership, their one hope of coping with the school board—the politicians—once again were declining to enter the fray.

The union's delegate body of course was unwilling to accept the school board's dismal interpretation of the situation. The board was accused of reneging, the union president was castigated for leaving a loophole in the contract, the politicians were urged to intervene, and all parties were put on notice that unless the original contract terms were restored, the teachers would strike. The delegates voted 314–14 in favor of full restoration of the contract terms, and on the following day the membership proved to be nearly as adamant, voting 16,500–3,653.

Yet instead of allowing the talks to drift into a strike as in the previous year, the leadership reached a compromise settlement with the board prior to the strike deadline. The terms of the settlement, however, were well below what the leadership had been directed to achieve. A salary increase of 5.5 percent was included in the agreement, but so was an eleven-day layoff and the elimination of 4,536 positions. In spite of fierce opposition, the leadership was able to push the compromise past the delegates with a 25-vote margin, 158–133. The union membership was not much more enthusiastic, voting 11,416–7,394 to accept the offer.

Thus, the leadership had courted disaster and survived. However, the compromise proved to be the moderate leadership's last hurrah. In preparation for the upcoming 1972 elections for union offices, the president's party dumped him. In his place the party slated a candidate who made the restoration of the original contract by means of an immediate strike his main campaign issue. Thus, after six years of moderate union rule, the leadership party was opting for a more fully developed form of union rule. The outcome of the party's dramatic change of candidates and commitment was that the new militant slate won by the same two-third's margin by which the moderate slate had won in the two preceding elections.[40]

Following the election of the new teacher union leadership, the pattern governing the collective-bargaining process took on a novel structure. The union leadership, rather than the politicians, now dictates the terms of the settlements. When the participation of the politicians is desired by the union leadership and the politicians decline to participate, the leadership will call a strike in order to force political intervention in the settlement process. The outcome of the new settlement-process pattern is that the union acquires far more benefits than it would if the determination of benefit levels were left to the politicians.[41]

The new pattern governing the settlement process was evident in the first negotiating session between the new union leadership and the board. The board entered the 1973 session facing a deficit of approximately $70 million. Nevertheless, the union submitted a request for a salary increase, albeit a modest one of 2.5 percent, a class size limitation to be imposed on all classrooms, and a one-week reduction in the school work year at no loss in salary. The leadership's position was endorsed by a membership vote of 16,525–2,979 to strike unless the union's demands were met.

The board responded by refusing to grant the demands. The union leadership, however, instead of reducing its demands as the moderate leadership invariably had done, made no move to compromise at all. The negotiating style of the new union leadership also differed dramatically. The newspapers carried accounts of hostile exchanges between the negotiating teams, whereas the moderate leadership had always gone out of its way to appear reasonable and conciliatory. Indeed, the union president even exchanged insults with Mayor Daley's primary spokesman on the school board, who had been a consistent supporter of the mayor's generous mediation on the teachers' behalf. Thus, Chicago's schools were struck for the third time; however, for the first time, the strike had the full support of the union leadership.

The 1973 strike proved to be as novel as the negotiating demands and style of the union leadership. Instead of moving in promptly to mediate, as he always had, Mayor Daley simply urged both parties to keep negotiating. Organized labor also turned its back on the teachers for the first time. School janitors and other service personnel, all affiliated with the Chicago Federation of Labor, were reported to be crossing the teachers' picket lines and working during the strike.[42] Yet in spite of the defection of the politicians and organized labor, the union leadership refused to compromise its demands, and the striking teachers maintained their strike at an efficiency level exceeding 90 percent.

Finally, after the strike had run for two weeks, Mayor Daley capitulated. He ordered the deadlocked parties to his office, mediation began, and then it turned out that even the mediation contained a novel twist. Previously, the mayor always had managed without much difficulty to convince at least a bare majority of the eleven-member school board to go along with a generous settlement. But this time the board balked. Daley was able to persuade only his four most loyal supporters on the board to accede to the union's demand for a shortened school year at no reduction in salary.[43]

The school board's unprecedented display of independence coupled with the union's refusal to moderate its demands proved to be too much for even the exceptional mediating skills of Mayor Daley. He stormed out of the mediation session to seek the aid of his fellow politicians in the city council. The council promptly approved a resolution authorizing the mayor to accept the resignations of all the sitting school board members. Daley himself added that he intended to accept the resignation of any board member who in his estimation was not making a sufficient effort to reach a settlement.[44]

On the day the mayor made his threat, the two additional votes came in, and thus the mayor had his way with the school board. As it turned out, the mayor's way was a settlement which included all of the union's orginal major demands plus a provision that allowed the teachers to make up seven of the twelve school days they had lost while striking.[45] Thus, the new militant union leadership had its way with Mayor Daley. In maintaining the strike, the union leadership showed that even a highly reluctant mayor could eventually be forced to intervene. In turn, by refusing to compromise, the leadership showed that even forced political intervention could produce the usual bountiful package of teacher benefits. The 1973 settlement, therefore, marks another major turning point in the city's school politics: the emergence of fully developed union rule.[46]

The following settlement session between the new union leadership and the school board, while it lacked the drama of the preceding session, nonetheless had its novel aspects too. As had now become a standard scenario, the board opened the 1974 talks by announcing that it faced an enormous deficit, this year's pegged at somewhat over $50 million. The union leadership in turn declared the deficit was due to mismanagement and faulty, misleading budgetary practices; that the teachers could not be expected to subsidize such a poorly managed system; and that, in any event, raising revenues for the schools was the board's responsibility, not the union's. The union leadership requested a salary increase of 11 percent.

This time, however, instead of flatly refusing to yield, the school board made a counteroffer of its own. The board proposed a salary increase of 4 percent. Their extraordinary decision was unquestionably irresponsible in view of the enormous deficit. Yet, a logic had come to govern the settlement process which actually encouraged and rewarded the board for behaving irresponsibly. The board properly calculated that if no salary increase were offered to the union, then the union would very likely strike and the strike would be followed by political intervention. The political intervention would in turn produce a settlement which was higher than the board was offering to avoid the strike. The board was opting for a slow boat to bankruptcy rather than a political express train engineered by the union and the mayor.[47]

However, the union leadership was being led by logic of its own, and turned down the school board's offer. Acceptance of the offer would have created the impression that accommodation had taken place, and the new union leadership was apparently intent upon distinguishing its militant style of leadership from its predecessor's moderate style. Accordingly, a strike vote was held, and by wide margins the delegates and the membership endorsed the leadership's decision to hold out for more. The delegates voted 304-2 and the membership 15,478-5,345.

Consequently, a strike seemed inevitable. Yet, instead of striking, the leadership reached a compromise settlement with the board. The settlement included a 5 percent salary increase along with a guarantee that the board would make no program cuts. No less surprising, since the leadership had extracted only an additional 1 percent increase in salary from the board, the delegates accepted the compromise with just one dissenting vote.

Thus, the new union leadership had achieved two unprecedented objectives. It had managed to secure a substantial increase in benefits without the aid of political mediation, and in the process the union leadership had shown that it, and not the school board, set the terms of settlement. No less important, the leadership had managed to virtually eliminate dissent within the union. Militancy, therefore, radically altered the internal as well as the external politics of the teachers' union.[48]

The very next year's negotiations serve to show just how radically altered school politics could become under a fully developed form of union rule. Presaging the adoption of a tougher bargaining style, the school board recruited a new school superintendent who was an ardent advocate of the restoration of a balanced budget. Inasmuch as the 1974 budget had soared over the $1-billion mark, accompanied by a deficit in excess of $100 million, the board apparently decided a fatalistic acceptance of deficits would not do after all. The media promptly billed the 1975 talks as a showdown between the new superintendent and the union for control of the city's schools.

One consequence of the militancy of the new superintendent was a heightening of the militancy of the already militant teachers. The union leadership presented the board and the superintendent with the largest set of demands the union had ever made: a cost-of-living salary increase, a reduction of class size in all classrooms, a paid dental insurance program, and make-up days for the length of time the teachers would have to strike in order to achieve their demands. The membership endorsed the unprecedented demands by an unprecedented vote of 89 percent, 21,439-2,537.[49]

The inevitable strike lasted eleven days and, in accordance with the new pattern governing the settlement process, ended in a novel manner but with predictable results. Mayor Daley, in response to the early urging of the union leadership for his intervention, advised the teachers to return to work and rely upon the state legislature's efforts to provide additional funds for the schools. The union leadership, of course, ignored the mayor's advice. Ultimately, the mayor had to intervene; however, he intervened this time in an entirely novel manner. Instead of calling in the two sides for mediation, Daley disrupted a social gathering of the school board, which ironically enough was being held to honor the new militant superintendent, to dictate the terms of a settlement to the assembled board members.

So ended the school board's brief fling with militancy. The terms of Mayor Daley's settlement proposal included all of the union's original main demands, and, as he had since he was first forced by the union to intervene in 1971, the mayor left the school board with the responsibility of finding the funds to finance the settlement. He also had concluded his interruption of the school board's social gathering by once again threatening any board members who remained uncooperative with dismissal.[50]

In response, seven of the school board's eleven members elected to abandon the superintendent's new get-tough policy in favor of the generous settlement proposed by the mayor. The financial consequences of the mayor's intervention this time left the school board with an estimated deficit of $135-150 million, and the prospect of restoring a balanced budget seemed far less likely than ever before. What the politicians and the school board obviously needed was an effective means of countering the teachers' union's almighty strike weapon. However, just what the means might consist of was not at all obvious.

Interestingly, some semblance of a countervailing force did surface in the following year's negotiation. The union leadership opened the 1976 talks with the astonishing announcement that rather than demanding its usual package of benefit increases, the union would settle for a simple extension of the 1975 contract. To be sure, the leadership's offer was not altogether moderate, for a contract extension entailed no cutbacks as well as no increases. In view of the difficulties that public unions elsewhere were encountering, the prime examples being in New York City, a contract without any cutbacks constituted a relative gain. Nevertheless, in terms of the standards which had been governing negotiations in Chicago since the new union leadership assumed office, the leadership's decision was remarkable.

However, the following year's negotiations revealed that the 1976 session simply was the exception that proves the rule. In 1977 the union received a two-year contract that provided back-to-back salary increases of 5 percent, and the contract called for no reductions in the school system workforce. The school board granted the increase even though it meant that the school system's deficit would remain hovering for the next two years around the $100-million mark.

Even more revealing in terms of the extent of influence the union has acquired in school affairs, the school board's action in 1977 mirrored its fatalistic 1974 behavior. It provided the union with a substantial benefit increase, accepted the inevitable massive deficit, and put up little of the resistance it typically had displayed before finally knuckling under to Mayor Daley's pro-union pressure during mediation.

This was the first contract session between the school board and the teachers' union during the administration of Mayor Bilandic, Daley's successor. If it is any indication of what is to come during the post-Daley period, it would appear that the union has established a stable position of dominance over the schools. The union will continue to extract sizable benefit increases, regardless of either the huge financial deficits entailed by such increases or the lack of any significant benefits for the school system's clientele.

One thing that is certain, however, is that the city's public school politics has come full circle by the late 1970s. At the turn of the century, the politicians were the undisputed primary beneficiary of the schools. Then, as reform rule eliminated the patronage incentives which had induced political participation in the schools, the politicians became indifferent to school affairs.

Now, with the emergence of union rule, the politicians once again are active participants in school politics. However, now their participation is not of their own choosing, nor is it intended primarily to advance their own interests. Instead, the politicians are being forced to participate by the unionized teachers, and the forced participation has served to make the teachers the undisputed primary beneficiary of the schools. Under union rule the politicians have become necessary but highly reluctant and largely helpless participants in the city's public school politics—much in the same way that the school children always have been. To the extent that politics has anything poetic about it, at that level at least some justice has been achieved.

Notes

1. Michael B. Katz, *Class, Bureaucracy, and Schools* (New York: Praeger Publications, 1975), p. 58.

2. The seminal contribution was the so-called Coleman Report by James S. Coleman, et al., *Equality of Educational Opportunity* (Washington, D.C.: Office of Education, 1966). A useful collection of commentary and reanalysis has been provided by Frederick Mosteller and Daniel P. Moynihan, eds., *On Equality of Educational Opportunity* (New York: Basic Books, 1972).

3. Colin Greer, *The Great School Legend* (New York: Basic Books, 1972).

4. The analytic device of prime beneficiary is drawn from Peter M. Blau and W. Richard Scott, *Formal Organizations: A Comparative Approach* (San Francisco: Chandler Publishing Co., 1962). As shown in table 1-1, Blau and Scott distinguished types of organizations on a basis of the organization's prime beneficiary. Here the device will be used to distinguish beneficiary conflict and succession as well.

5. James S. Coleman has very effectively criticized this viewpoint in an essay stressing the significance of communication in the relationship between organizations and their consumers. See his *Power and the Structure of Society* (New York: W.W. Norton & Co., 1974).

6. In this regard, James Q. Wilson has remarked that "The best empirical political science has, in my view, usually (not always) been that which has tried to explain why one goal rather than another is served by government,

and the consequences of serving that goal, or serving it in a particular way. Such a concern draws together the empirical and philosophical aspects of political inquiry . . . . (Introduction: City Politics and Public Policy," In James Q. Wilson, ed., *City Politics and Public Policy* [New York: John Wiley and Sons, 1968] , p. 3.)

7. For a useful overview, based on many of the standard reference works, see Joseph M. Cronin, *The Control of Urban Schools: Perspective on the Power of Educational Reformers* (New York: Free Press, 1973).

8. An excellent general study of school reform has been made by Raymond Callahan, *Education and the Cult of Efficiency* (Chicago: University of Chicago Press, 1962). The early Chicago school reform situation has been investigated in a classic study of school politics by George S. Counts, *School and Society in Chicago* (New York: Harcourt, Brace and Co., 1928).

9. The observation was made privately by President John Desmond of the Chicago Teachers' Union. Publicly, Desmond usually insisted that the purpose of collective bargaining was to improve the educational quality of the schools, and that salaries were a secondary consideration. Both sides of Desmond's rhetoric are contained in an excellent study of Chicago's school politics by Paul E. Peterson, *School Politics: Chicago Style* (Chicago: University of Chicago Press, 1976), p. 197.

10. The statement was made by one of the American Federation of Teachers' national organizers, and is contained in Robert J. Braun, *Teachers and Power: The Story of the American Federation of Teachers* (New York: Simon and Schuster, Touchstone Book, 1972). For additional viewpoints on the objectives of the teachers' unions, see the sources cited in chapter 1, note 4.

11. The rise of public employee organization influence during the late 1950s and early 1960s is discussed respectively in Wallace S. Sayre and Herbert Kaufman, *Governing New York City* (New York: W.W. Norton & Co., 1965), and Theodore Lowi, "Gosnell's Chicago Revisited via Lindsey's New York," foreword to the second edition, in Harold F. Gosnell, *Machine Politics: Chicago Model* (Chicago: University of Chicago Press, 1968). For an excellent account of the devastating impact the public employee unions have had on the cities since coming to power, see Norton E. Long, *The Unwalled City: Reconstituting the Urban Community* (New York: Basic Books, 1972).

12. Public employees now represent organized labor's principal growth sector. The development is outlined in Sterling Spero and John M. Capozzola, *The Union Community and Its Unionized Bureaucracies: Pressure Politics in Local Government Labor Relations* (New York: Dunellen, 1973), pp. 13-39.

13. Mary J. Herrick, *The Chicago Schools: A Social and Political History* (Beverly Hills, Cal.: Sage Publications, 1971), p. 50.

14. The following account draws on Herrick, *Chicago Schools.* Two excellent additional sources are Counts, *School and Society,* and Charles E. Merriam,

Chicago: A More Intimate View of Urban Politics (New York: Macmillan Co., 1929). Sol Cohen provides a description of New York City school politics during the same period, which in broad outline follows the developments in Chicago. See *Progressives and Urban School Reform: 1895-1954* (New York: Columbia University Press, 1964).

15. Herrick, *Chicago Schools,* p. 141.

16. The three criteria can be found in the seminal writings of Max Weber on the modern bureaucracy and in the works of any number of later writers who have extended Weber's analysis.

17. Herrick's *Chicago Schools* has been used to provide the details for the reform period. Count's *School and Society* contains a valuable account of the McAndrew superintendency. An excellent general source is Callahan, *Education and Efficiency.*

18. Cohen, *Progressives and Reform,* describes how the New York City political machine capitalized on the school reformers' support of the Gary Plan to drive the reformers from City Hall after a single term of office.

19. The reform did not, however, hold up over time. According to a knowledgeable source, today there is "massive patronage in the nonteaching personnel of the school system." See Milton Rakove, *Don't Make No Waves: Don't Back No Losers* (Bloomington: Indiana University Press, 1975), pp. 205-206. Apparently, Superintendent Hunt and Mayor Kennelly were able to place their reformers in key positions while the scandal intimidated the machine politicans; however, as the scandal receded, the politicians were able to reassert their traditional hegemony.

20. Benjamin C. Willis, "The Need for Professionalism in Education Today," *Chicago Schools Journal,* March 1954. Cited in Herrick, *Chicago Schools.*

21. *Proceedings of the Chicago Board of Education,* April 23, 1964. Joseph Pois, a school board member during part of the Willis administration, has described the autocratic nature of Superintendent Willis. See *The School Board Crisis: A Chicago Case Study* (Chicago: Educational Methods, 1964).

22. Willis's loss of business-community support is documented in Stephen D. London, *Business and the Chicago Public School System, 1890-1966* (Ph.D. dissertation, University of Chicago, 1968).

23. The principles were stated by a former long-term ward committeeman of a notorious Chicago "river ward," Bernie Neistein. Cited in Rakove, *Don't Make No Waves.*

24. According to one of the school board members,

> All the good board members who normally vote as a bloc with the establishment were adamant against granting the union the right of collective bargaining. . . . Bill Lee (president of the Chicago Federation of Labor) and one or two other top leaders very closely identified with the so-called "power structure" of this city were sent over to the Board meetings, and those Board members who were adamant against granting the union this right changed just like that."

Warren Bacon, "Comments," in Sol Tax, ed., *The People vs. the System: A Dialogue in Union Conflict* (Chicago: Acme Press, 1968), p. 167. Cited in Peterson, *School Politics*, p. 283.

25. The following account is drawn from local newspaper accounts. Herrick's *Chicago Schools* contains no mention of the union leadership's behavior during this critical turning point in school and union politics. In general, her treatment of the union after it acquired collective-bargaining rights is inadequate. Herrick was a teacher-union activist and an ardent reformer while she taught in the Chicago public schools.

26. The American Federation of Teachers repealed its no-strike pledge at its 1963 annual convention. Thus, the Chicago union leadership clearly was out of line with AFT policy. Alan Rosenthal has shown just how conservative the Chicago Teachers' Union leadership was at this point in the union's development. See his "Pedagogues and Power," *Urban Affairs Quarterly* 2 (September 1966), pp. 83–102.

27. The president was John Fewkes, who has been described as the "John L. Lewis of the teacher labor movement." Robert Braun describes some of Fewkes's militant activities in his younger, radical days in *Teachers and Power: The Story of the American Federation of Teachers* (New York: Simon and Schuster, Touchstone Book, 1972), pp. 42–48.

28. The Chicago Federation of Labor vote is recorded in the *Chicago Sun Times,* September 23, 1965. The personal intercession of President Lee with Mayor Daley is reported by J. David Greenstone, *Labor in American Politics* (New York: Alfred A. Knopf, 1968), pp. 94–95.

29. The remarkable transformation of the United Federation of Teachers has been described by Braun, *Teachers and Power,* pp. 60–66.

30. Refer to note 24.

31. Despite the electoral dominance of President John Fewkes, the Chicago Teachers' Union experienced much organizational conflict with other teachers' groups. Fewkes's close ally and successor, John Desmond, gained the presidency by only 116 votes in 1966. Desmond continued to be beset by internal conflict until he was driven from office by his own party in 1972. This is discussed in more detail shortly.

32. The benefits are contained in the *Agreement between the Chicago Board of Education and the Chicago Teachers' Union* for the years in question. The teachers' benefits are more fully described in chapter 3.

33. A patronage system essentially secures compliance through coercion, whereas a collective-bargaining system relies on monetary rewards to secure compliance. An excellent treatment of compliance relationships is provided by Amitai W. Etzioni, *A Comparative Analysis of Complex Organizations* (New York: Free Press, 1961).

34. Contract negotiations finally were shifted to the fall in 1974, which enabled the negotiations to take place on a basis of actual rather than anticipated revenues.

35. The union votes cited throughout this chapter are drawn from one or both of two sources: local newspaper accounts and *Chicago Union Teacher,* the union's monthly newspaper.

36. The salary increases reported here are "average" increases. Newspapers typically report salary increases for entry-level teachers only. However, this is often very misleading. The union usually negotiates varying salary increases for senior, mid-level, and entering teachers. Thus, the midpoint between minimum and maximum salaries for teachers with the B.A. degree was used here to more accurately reflect the union's gains in salary increases. The procedure is further specified in chapter 3, note 10.

37. *Chicago Sun Times,* May 23, 1969.

38. Ibid., January 12, 1970.

39. The teacher union leadership's acceptance of the contingency provision in the 1971 contract is further evidence of its moderate objectives as well as its naïveté. Since Daley was not willing to accept responsibility for securing the funds needed to finance the settlement, there was very little likelihood that the 1972 salary increase would be forthcoming. This, in turn, left the union leadership hopelessly out on a limb.

40. The new union president paved his way to the presidency in the classic Chicago manner: everyone in his way got paid off to get out of his way. The incumbent president decided he would not run as an independent candidate without party support after being given a lobbyist job with the union at a salary in excess of $30,000. The presidential and vice-presidential candidates of the leading opposition party also dropped out of the election and wound up on the union's payroll, one as a field services representative and the other as editor of the union's monthly newspaper. A current union official provided me with this information, but declined to be named in this note.

41. By this time, the politicians' support for the teachers had declined considerably. Mayor Daley had not voluntarily intervened since 1969, and he was no longer willing to assume the responsibility he once had for securing additional funding to finance teacher benefit increases.

42. *Chicago Sun Times,* January 11, 1973.

43. Voting records of all the school board members on the collective-bargaining contracts are contained in table 5-2.

44. *Chicago Sun Times,* January 25, 1973.

45. Ibid., January 26, 1973.

46. Responding to a reporter's question as to how the funds would be found to finance the substantial 1973 settlement mediated by the mayor, the union president provided what might well be the motto of fully developed union rule: "I didn't ask." *Chicago Sun Times,* January 26, 1973.

47. One board member, Bernard Friedman, had observed, "Our experience has been that when we have gone to the mayor's office, we have ended up giving more than we had planned to." *Chicago Sun Times,* January 13, 1970.

48. In 1974 and 1976 the incumbent union officers were not challenged by even a token opposition slate, ending a long history of multipartyism in the schools. Thus, the Chicago Teachers' Union has come to finally resemble the more typical, oligarchically structured unions described by Grant McConnell, *Private Power and American Democracy* (New York: Alfred A. Knopf, 1966).

49. The size of this vote reflects the enormous growth of the Chicago Teachers' Union since it acquired collective bargaining rights. In 1965, union membership was 13,063; by 1975, membership had risen to 29,021. Much of the increase is due to an expansion of the union's recruitment base. In 1967 the union won the right to represent the school system's clerical workers and some paraprofessionals. Teacher aides were added to the bargaining unit in 1971. Assistant principals also are members of the CTU. Data on the union's membership through 1976 is contained in Marion Byrnes and Nicholas Cannella, *136 Years of Teaching in Chicago* (Chicago: Chicago Teachers' Union, no date).

50. *Chicago Sun Times,* September 18, 1975.

3

Union Rule in the Big-City Bureaucracy

Introduction

Political science, in a classic formulation by Harold Lasswell, was defined as the study of "who gets what, when, how." In elaborating his thesis, Lasswell distinguishes an elite as "those who get the most of what there is to get." In turn, "a shift in the class composition of elites" constitutes a revolution.[1]

Notwithstanding the considerable deference accorded to Lasswell's study since its publication in 1936, only recently have political scientists actually gotten around to focusing upon the "what" in his classic definition. Under the rubric of "public-policy analysis," since the late 1960s a number of studies have been concerned principally with identifying and accounting for the outputs of politics. However, these studies generally have defined "what" in terms of financial expenditure levels, rather than using the broader and more substantive range of values and benefits outlined by Lasswell.[2] As for revolutions, generally they still are considered to be massive, noisy, and wracking affairs, and therefore are regarded as phenomena occurring mainly in historical times and nowadays only in underdeveloped places.

In this chapter and the following two, we shall use Lasswell's classic definition as a general framework for a comparative analysis of union rule. In doing so, it should become evident that a new elite, the unionized employees of the public bureaucracies, is emerging in big-city politics. In turn, to the extent it can be shown that the unionized public employees are displacing the traditional elites of big-city school politics—the politicians and the school managers—it should be no less evident that a revolution is occurring in big-city politics.

The general subject of this chapter is who gets what under union rule. Specifically, we shall analyze the benefits acquired by Chicago's public school teachers as a result of collective bargaining. The analysis of benefits conducted here differs from other analyses of educational public policy in two significant respects. First, we shall compare the benefits acquired by Chicago's public school teachers under union rule with the benefits they acquired under machine and reform rule, respectively. Typically, the comparative framework which has been used involved a comparison among different localities rather than different forms of government.[3]

The method of comparison used here has several distinct advantages. It obviously enables us to evaluate changes in the distribution of benefits which have occurred over time, which of course cannot be accomplished by the conventional method of comparing benefits acquired contemporaneously in different local-ities. The historical dimension thus uniquely affords benchmarks enabling us to more properly assess the amount and types of benefits which currently are being acquired. When we therefore speak of increases and changes, we shall be doing so within a particular and concrete frame of reference.

More important, our comparative method relates differences in public policy to three distinct forms of urban government. This again is a dimension which a time-bound method of analysis is highly unlikely to uncover. The differences among contemporary forms of government are simply not as distinct. The in-formation derived from this method of analysis therefore enables a more in-formed judgment as to how particular changes in governmental form correspond to significantly different public policies.[4]

Indeed, as we shall see, the differences in benefits acquired by Chicago's school teachers under each of the three forms of urban government have been considerable and highly distinctive. Under machine rule, Chicago's teachers were a part of the city's great under class, lacking both economic and political status. With the emergence of reform rule, the teachers were able to make considerable economic gains; however, their political influence remained as inconsequential as ever. Under union rule, the teachers have made even greater economic gains, and they have become a part of the city's political elite as well.

The second respect in which the analysis here differs from other analyses of school policy is that a broad range of policies is taken into consideration. In general, studies of public policy have focused upon financial expenditure levels, in effect using the gross distribution of dollars as a surrogate for the more particular distribution of benefits and services. Moreover, those school policy studies which have had a more substantive distributive orientation usually have concentrated on only one or a few highly controversial policies, such as com-munity control and desegregation.[5]

The problem with the general approach is that by focusing upon financial expenditures, little consideration is given to the substantive aspects of public policy. Then, by using the level of expenditures as an indicator of policy changes, little knowledge is gained about the distributive aspects of public policy. The problem with the more substantive school-policy studies is that it is difficult to make inferences on the basis of only one or a few policy indicators. Indeed, it becomes even more difficult to do so when volatile issues such as community control and desegregation are used as indicators. Such policies frequently have in-duced "siege" rather than normal behavior on the part of the school participants.

What we shall do here, then, is focus upon the broad gamut of school policies covered by the collective-bargaining agreements produced by the school board and the teachers' union. These agreements provide us with a large and highly varied set of policy indicators, which enable us to more confidently draw conclusions concerning the primary beneficiaries of the city's school politics. The agreements reached by the board and the union involve a number of critical substantive issues, such as performance accountability, limitations on client and managerial access to school benefits, and tenure and termination procedures. A number of the agreement indicators also provide us with information not only about who benefits from the city's public schools, but who makes the determinations as to who will benefit and the means by which such determinations are made. Finally, because the collective-bargaining process is a normal and regularly recurring event, we are better able to determine how policy typically is established and to whose advantage the city's public schools commonly are geared.

The several policies analyzed here are all contained in the contracts reached between the Chicago Board of Education and the Chicago Teachers' Union. For the sake of clarity, the policies will be considered under four general categories: salary and related benefits, employment security, working conditions, and managerial and educational policy. Although we are looking here at Chicago school policies, the substance of the policies under consideration should not vary to any great degree from one city to another. This is because both the American Federation of Teachers and the National Education Association have produced "basic model agreements." The models produced by these two national organizations contain standard provisions, including specific wording, for inclusion in the contracts negotiated by local teachers' unions. Indeed, the model agreements of the AFT and the NEA do not differ much beyond the wording of specific provisions. Consequently, big-city, town, and countryside school boards all face remarkably similar bargaining demands from their local school teachers.[6]

Salary and Related Benefits

"They had three demands: they were money, money, money."[7] So observed one member of the Chicago school board at the conclusion of a negotiating session with the teachers' union. The president of the Chicago Teachers' Union of course denied the charge. After all, it would not do to publicly agree with the "bosses" or to openly acknowledge the pecuniary preoccupations of the teachers. Yet in private, the union leader revealed that the board member had correctly described the union's bargaining agenda. Shortly after the teachers' union had won the right to collectively bargain with the school board, the president confided, "Salaries are the first thing. I want to get the highest salaries in the country. Then, we can work on class size."[8]

Aside from the remarkable achievement of the Chicago Teachers' Union, it is important to recognize how the viewpoints of the two antagonists do coincide. As table 3-1 indicates, Chicago's teachers are indeed at the head of the class in terms of salary. The union president distinguished class size as a separate, secondary consideration, one of a number of improvements in working conditions to be dealt with after salary increases had been secured. Yet, from the school board's point of view, both policies amount to the same thing in one

Table 3-1

Teacher Salary and Real Income Comparison: Six Major Cities, Fall 1975

Salary Level	Chicago	New York	Philadelphia	Los Angeles	Houston	Detroit
Minimum (B.A.)	$11,138	$ 9,700	$ 8,900	$ 8,900	$ 9,300	$10,308
Real income	7,123	5,872	5,138	5,680	5,762	6,447
Maximum (B.A.)	19,642	16,650	16,466	14,130	13,300	17,516
Real income	12,551	10,079	10,071	9,017	8,860	10,954
Years to attain						
maximum salary	15	10	11	9	14	11

Source: Report of the Governor's Task Force on School Finance (Springfield, Ill.: Office of the Governor, 1975).

crucial respect: money. Thus, although in this section money is dealt with directly in terms of salary and related benefits, it must be borne in mind that money is the common denominator of a good many policies sought by the teachers' union. This is because education is a labor-intensive industry. Indeed, when a teachers' union has secured the right to negotiate on salary scales and class sizes, it has secured the right to make decisions concerning approximately 80 percent of the school system's educational budget.[9]

The current achievements of the Chicago teachers, compared to teachers in other major cities, are therefore impressive. However, these achievements are modest compared to the gains which Chicago's teachers have made since machine rule and reform rule, respectively. Figure 3-1 indicates the average salaries which the Chicago public school teachers received under each of the three forms of urban government.[10]

Under the first form of urban government, machine rule, the schools predominantly were under political control, and the Chicago political organization was at the zenith of its power during this period. As figure 3-1 makes abundantly clear, the machine politicians paid little interest to the teachers' monetary needs. Indeed, if a straight line is drawn between the 1928 and 1944 income levels, it can be seen that the teachers made virtually no gains in salary or real income under machine rule.

However, once the schools came under reform rule in 1946, teacher fortunes took an abrupt swing upward, and thereafter both salary and real income continued to increase progressively. As we noted earlier, during reform rule the schools began operating independently of the city's political system for the first time. It is, then, quite apparent that an autonomous school board and management served teacher interests much more effectively than had the politicians.

Of additional interest about this segment of the figure is that in 1955 Richard J. Daley was elected mayor, and he served as mayor until 1976. Note, on the one hand, that Daley's election had no impact whatsoever on teacher

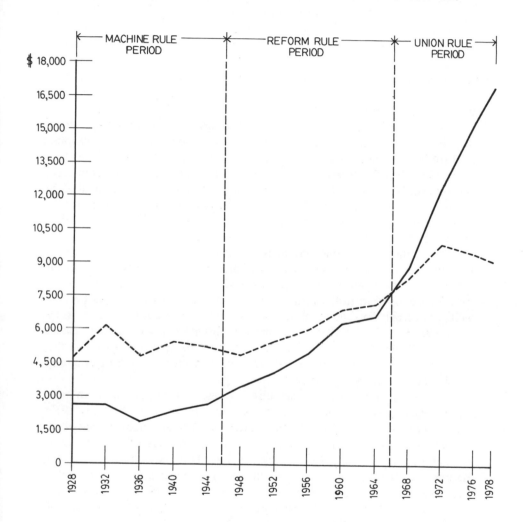

Source: Marion Byrnes and Nicholas Cannella, *136 Years of Teaching in Chicago* (Chicago: Chicago Teachers' Union, no date).

Figure 3–1. Chicago Teacher Salary and Income Comparison: Three Forms of Urban Rule, 1928–1978

fortunes; nothing changed until the teachers acquired collective-bargaining rights in 1966. On the other hand, look at how different the Daley political machine's relationship to teacher monetary interests is, during both the reform- and union-rule periods, compared to the earlier machine-rule relationship. Thus, it is evident that the machine's relationship to the teachers has been attenuated significantly by both reform rule and union rule, only far more so by the latter.

With the onset of union rule, teachers' salaries soared at an unprecedented rate to unprecedented levels. Clearly, given the inflationary trend which is shown by figure 3-1, if salaries had continued to increase at the reform-rule rate, the real income of the teachers would not have risen beyond the 1966 level by 1976. The teachers' acquisition of collective-bargaining rights was, therefore, not only highly beneficial, but quite timely as well.

In addition to salary, public school teachers receive a number of fringe benefits, such as holidays and sick leave with pay, and health and life insurance paid for by the school board. Thus, figure 3-1 does not reflect the full package of monetary benefits received by the teachers during the three periods of urban government. While it is difficult to assign an exact monetary value to all of the income-related benefits, they merit some discussion in order to sketch a more comprehensive picture of the monetary gains the teachers made under each of the forms of urban rule.

During the machine-rule period, as low as salary and real income were, the full monetary package received by the teachers often was lower than the amount indicated by the figure. The salaries which the teachers received, for example, were frequently paid in the form of "scrip." A number of businesses were unwilling to accept the scrip at all, and others would not accept the scrip at its full face value. Additionally, there were numerous, often lengthy periods of "payless paydays." While the teachers eventually received the back pay to which they were entitled, in the intervening periods they frequently had to borrow money, which required payment of interest.

In addition, a number of fringe benefits were curtailed during much of the machine-rule period. Sick leave with pay was withdrawn during the early 1930s, and the benefit was not fully restored until 1946. The paid-holiday benefit also was withdrawn for a period of time. Of course, times were not easy for many employees, public or otherwise, during the Great Depression. However, as Mary Herrick documents in her history of the Chicago public schools, the teachers were singled out for particularly oppressive treatment by the politicians because they were not within the politicians' patronage system to the extent that other public employees were.[11]

By the succeeding period of reform rule, all of the teachers' fringe benefits had been restored. Moreover, most of the benefits were liberalized during the reform period. For example, the school board traditionally allowed a limited number of sick-leave days to accumulate beyond a school year in order to accommodate a serious illness. At the outset of the reform-rule period, the cumulative total was raised to fifteen days. By 1955, the cumulative total had been increased to thirty days, while the amount of paid sick leave per year was raised from five to ten days. Three years later, the cumulative total was increased to ninety days. All in all, though, given the limited scope of fringe-benefit entitlements, the salary and real income levels of the reform-rule period, as indicated by figure 3-1, closely approximate the full teacher monetary benefit package.[12]

By contrast, the salary and real income levels for the union-rule period substantially understate the full monetary benefit package received by the teachers. Under union rule, all of the standard fringe benefits were significantly expanded, and a good many other fringe benefits were created, the likes of which went well beyond even the fondest contemplations of the reform-rule teachers and certainly those of the machine-rule period.

The grandest fringe benefit created by the union-rule teachers involves insurance protection. Things started off modestly enough. As a result of the first contract settlement, the teachers received a fully paid individual Blue Cross–Blue Shield insurance policy. While this was no meager fringe benefit in itself, by 1975 the school board had agreed to pay the full cost of a family health insurance policy, and at benefit levels which had been twice extended. Additionally, the school board was providing a life insurance plan as well as a dental insurance plan at no cost to the teachers. As one union official reportedly remarked, it had become easy to pick teachers out of a crowd by the mid-1970s: all you had to do was check the teeth of the crowd. The amount appropriated by the school board to pay for the insurance fringe benefit in 1975 exceeded $18 million.[13]

In addition to expanding all existing fringe benefits and creating some entirely new ones, the union also modified the concept and purpose of the cumulative sick-pay policy. The cumulative sick-pay policy was, as we said, a form of insurance that was to be applied in the event of an illness extending beyond the provisions of the annual sick-leave policy. During the reform-rule period, the policy had been enlarged from two weeks to approximately one-half of the school year. During union rule, the cumulative sick-pay provision was extended to 200 days, which is in excess of one school year.

Additionally, the sick-leave concept has been expanded into a retirement benefit as well. The board–union contract now provides for the receipt upon retirement of one-half of a teacher's accumulated sick leave in the form of a cash payment. The school board justifies this benefit arguing that it reduces abuse of the sick-leave provision by teachers. When a teacher is sick during the course of a school year, the board must pay both the teacher and the salary of a substitute teacher, yet the amount of teaching a substitute generally can accomplish is less than that of a regular classroom teacher. It is, in any event, a very expensive fringe benefit.[14]

Employment Security

If salary comes first from the teacher union's point of view, considerations of job security certainly do not run far behind. From the public's point of view, however, job security should rank ahead of salary as a consideration. For it is one thing to provide costly salary and fringe benefits as long as the job is being performed well. Yet, it is something else altogether to incur the same expense while being saddled with employees who are so secure in their employment that, regardless of the return they provide on the public's investment, little can be done to alter their productive effort. Such, as we shall see, has come to be the case with the union-rule teachers.

Performance accountability always has been a serious problem in the big-city public schools. During the machine-rule period, educational accountability typically was defined in terms of cost rather than productivity.[15] Thus, a school which was serving its clientele at a lower per capita rate was considered superior to other more costly schools, regardless of how much the clientele was learning in a given school. Because the schools fell within the politicians' patronage system of employment, educational personnel (from the classroom teacher on up to the superintendent) were more likely to be evaluated in terms of how well they met the needs of their political sponsor rather than the needs of the schools' clientele.

When the reformers took over the schools, they too employed measures of accountability which managed to ignore productivity. The quality of a given school came to be measured in terms of a wide array of professionally established criteria.[16] Thus, a school that employed teachers having bachelors degrees typically was regarded as better than a school using teachers with only two-year degrees acquired from the normal schools, but it was not as good as a school that boasted of teachers with masters degrees. The variety of professional personnel a school employed also was highly valued. Counselors, testers of various sorts, specialists of one kind and another—all came to be seen as means of assessing the worth of a school. Even the number of volumes in a school library was used to evaluate schools, regardless of how well the students could read the books. While the reformers were greatly expanding the educational enterprise, they also managed to institute a system of peer evaluation. This effectively reduced the status of any external analysis and commentary on the schools to that of uninformed lay observation.

Big-city union-rule educators have come to deal with performance accountability in an altogether different manner. Rather than using the per capita cost or the presumed effectiveness of certain educational inputs, the union-rule educators argue that they cannot be held responsible for what is accomplished in the schools. Student cultural deprivation was the argument of absolution used by educators during the 1960s. During the 1970s, lack of adequate funding and lack of parental concern have been made to shoulder their share of the blame for poor school performance.

Two other stumbling blocks to accountability recently have received a good deal of attention from the educators. It turns out that the tests which the schools have been relying upon to measure productivity (not the educators', of course, but the students'), are culturally rigged in favor of the white middle class. Therefore, particularly in regard to the inner-city schools, the tests are invalid. Perhaps to hedge against the possibility of a scientific breakthrough in test development, the educators also are beginning to emphasize that schooling consists of a great variety of learnings. Many of the subjects defy precise measurement: civic virtue, integrity, love of honor, to mention just a few. As a result, even in those schools where virtually none of the students are learning to read and write, a good deal of education may be taking place.

The educators have not always had it so good, however. During the period of machine rule, employment security was a very serious problem. During reform rule, the problem improved but by no means disappeared. During both periods of urban government, a significant number of teachers were dismissed for either "good cause," to use the language of the contract, or poor performance. Table 3-2 lists the number of formal teacher terminations from the Chicago public schools during each of the periods of urban government.

In addition to formal terminations, teachers are subject to various other pressures to resign from the school system. While a precise number of such dismissals cannot be ascertained, from what we know about the personnel practices of each of the periods of urban government, some reasonable conclusions can be drawn. Under machine rule, the teachers had both political and managerial pressures with which to contend, and the political pressure was considerable. Patronage appointments are tied closely to electoral success, and so as political fortunes shifted, so too did the employment prospects of those teachers subject to the politicians' patronage system. The tenure law of 1917 afforded the teachers some protection, but until the teachers passed the three-year probationary period, they possessed limited security.

As the school system became reformed, the political pressure to which the teachers had been subjected greatly subsided. However, managerial discretion

Table 3-2
Formal Teacher Terminations from the Chicago Public Schools, 1933-1971

Time Period	Number of Terminations	Annual Average
1933-1946 (Machine rule)	316	22.6
1947-1966 (Reform rule)	132	6.6
1967-1971 (Union rule)	3	0.6

Sources: For 1933-1946, *Proceedings of the Chicago Board of Education;* for 1947-1971, *Facts and Figures: The Chicago Public Schools* (Chicago: Board of Education).

was still very much in force. Consequently, it can be inferred that there was a decline in informal terminations, although the teachers very likely were still under a good deal of pressure because of considerable unilateral managerial authority.

Under union rule, on the other hand, both political and managerial discretion are reduced considerably. Reform rule reduced political influence over the teachers; union rule, in turn, reduces managerial influence. Therefore, the performance of the teachers is no longer subject to any significant influence. Since the advent of collective bargaining, the teachers have been afforded the highly effective protection of an elaborate, precise, and time-consuming performance evaluation procedure. The outcome of the procedure is that fewer teachers are likely to receive a performance rating low enough to subject them to the prospect of termination.

The following list summarizes the evaluation procedure used in the case of a tenured teacher whom a school principal considers to be performing at an unsatisfactory level.[17]

1. The principal initiates the procedure by informing the teacher in writing of an unsatisfactory performance. The notice must be given at a private consultation.

2. The notification and the consultation must include specific suggestions as to how the teacher's performance can be upgraded, and the principal must provide additional assistance.

3. During the following ten weeks, the principal must confer with the teacher no less than three times, and each conference must include additional suggestions for removing the unsatisfactory rating.

4. During this same time, the district superintendent must confer with the teacher at least once, and he too must make suggestions as to how the unsatisfactory rating may be removed. A conference with the area superintendent (the Chicago school system is divided into three areas) is stipulated as optional.

5. By the fifty-first school day, the principal must issue a second notice of continuing unsatisfactory performance. Otherwise, the process terminates automatically.

6. Following the second notice, a final conference must be held. The conferees include the teacher, principal, area superintendent, assistant superintendent for personnel and/or the director of teacher personnel.

7. The general superintendent receives the recommendation of the conference participants.

Thus, it is hardly surprising that very few union-rule teachers are being terminated as a result of unsatisfactory performance. As elaborate as the procedure is, it actually comprises only a part of the full termination process.

According to an official of the Chicago Assistant Principals' Association, the entire process typically requires one school year. Most of the time is devoted to building a lengthy and well-documented case, and this must be done by the school principal alone, since he is the only individual with the authority to evaluate teachers. The official stated that it would be difficult to process more than one or two cases a year. Furthermore, higher school officials discourage principals from using the procedure on a regular basis.[18]

What usually happens, then, is that dissatisfied school principals and teachers resort to a form of "plea bargaining." A principal advises a teacher who is regarded as unsatisfactory that he will be subjected to various forms of harassment, including if necessary the formal procedure outlined above, unless the teacher agrees to transfer to another school. This arrangement of course saves the local manager from a time-consuming and thankless task, the teacher is saved from an unsatisfactory performance rating, and neither party bears much system-wide concern over the effects of the negotiated transfer of incompetent teachers. A final crucial consideration is that according to the Chicago school super-intendent, it costs the school board approximately $25,000 to terminate a teacher who avails himself of all the legal remedies provided him by the school system.

In addition to the evaluation-procedure safeguard, teachers also have re-course to the grievance procedure at any time. As it was originally conceived, a grievance procedure was supposed to serve as a substitute for legal redress in a court of law. Therefore, grievances were intended to be confined to matters covered within the contractual agreement. If the scope of matters covered by the grievance procedure is broader than the terms of the contract, then of course a teacher may use the law courts as well as the grievance procedure for the same offense. Nevertheless, the Chicago contract states that a grievance may be filed concerning any and all school policies and practices. The outcome of this extraordinary provision in the contract is that any school principal intending to actively supervise his teachers must be thoroughly conversant with the terms of the board–union contract, and the way in which the terms have been inter-preted in the courts and by the arbitrators. Otherwise, he may well wind up in court himself.[19]

Working Conditions

As we said earlier, it often is difficult to improve working conditions in a labor-intensive industry such as education without investing considerable sums of money. Moreover, it may be difficult to specify just what educational advantage is obtained (not to mention how much) by improving a given working condition. Reductions in class size represent the classic instance of this situation. The teachers' unions defend the need to reduce class size on the grounds that not only is a reduction an improvement in working conditions, but it represents an educational gain as well. This is simply to argue: students learn more in smaller classes.

The argument seems intuitively plausible in the extreme instances. Twenty students are better than fifty students in a classroom, if only because classroom-management duties and problems diminish, leaving more time to devote to instruction. Yet, plausibility wanes when it comes to smaller reductions, say from 30 to 28, which is the level around which a number of teachers' unions and school boards now are niggling. As for evidence to support the argument, it is inconclusive. Indeed, given the many variables and difficult measurements which are involved, the jury is likely to remain out a long while.

If the educational advantages of reductions in class size remain a mystery, the costs associated with reductions certainly are clear enough. Consider a reduction from 30 to 28 students in a school population approximately the size of Chicago's, 500,000. Using thirty-student units, the required number of classroom teachers is 16,666. A reduction of the student unit by two increases the required number of teachers by nearly 1,200. At the going rate for new Chicago teachers, the cash outlay for a two-students-per-class reduction therefore exceeds $13 million. That constitutes an exceedingly costly investment for an indeterminant, presumably minor educational gain. When the strapped financial condition of the big-city public schools is taken into consideration, the investment becomes all the more difficult to justify.

Class-size reductions, nevertheless, continue to be ever present in board–union negotiations, and classes are getting smaller year after year. During the 1920s, Chicago's elementary schools had an average class size of 45.5 students. At the outset of the reform-rule period, the average had decreased to 39.7. However, neither of these figures reflects a true average size, because nonclassroom teachers are included in the calculation. Thus, the actual average is higher than reported in both instances.[20]

Accordingly, the teachers' union negotiates on a basis of maximum class-size levels. In 1975, the Chicago Teachers' Union reached an agreement with the school board that no kindergarten or primary grade classroom could contain more than 29 students. The maximum level established for the intermediate grades was 32 students. For the majority of high school classes, the maximum was set at 28 students. As an indication of the overall financial impact of these continual reductions in class size, between 1973 and 1975, student enrollment in the Chicago public schools declined by 35,000. The corresponding decrease in staff, however, numbered only 56, whereas if staff had been reduced proportionately, the reduction would have been approximately 3,000. Calculated conservatively, the difference in salary costs alone exceeds $30 million.[21]

The union-rule teachers thus are required to serve fewer and fewer students, and far fewer than their machine-rule and reform-rule counterparts. At the same time, union-rule teachers have secured more and more help in meeting their reduced obligations. A policy which comes up regularly at the contract negotiating sessions between the school board and the union is the number of additional staff the board will hire in order to reduce the workload of the currently employed teaching staff.

In the first contract negotiated by the Chicago Teachers' Union, the school board agreed to hire 1,200 teacher aides in order to relieve the teachers of clerical and other nonprofessional duties, and to provide the teachers with more time for so-called "self-directed professional activities." The following year, the board agreed to hire an additional 600 teacher aides, and the next year 725 more teachers were hired to further reduce class size.[22]

In 1975, the year in which the Chicago school system's financial deficit went over the $100-million level for the first time, the school board nevertheless agreed to employ a special cadre of 600 permanent substitute teachers. These permanent substitutes were in addition to the nearly 1,200 substitutes already employed on a day-to-day basis. The special cadre was hired so that regularly employed teachers no longer would be required to cover classrooms that were left temporarily vacant by teachers on sick leave or personal business leave.

One other policy involving working conditions merits some attention. The policy pertains to student discipline procedures and rights. The policy is particularly noteworthy because it represents in microcosm the increasing disregard of the teachers' union toward the rights of both school clientele and school management. The policy states that upon a teacher's recommendation, a student who is deemed disruptive shall be removed from the classroom. Then, in order to return, the school principal is required to provide the student with consultation in the presence of the teacher. After two additional dismissals, the principal must call in both the student and his parents for consultation, again in the teacher's presence, before the student can return to class. Finally, if in the teacher's estimation the student remains disruptive, the principal must suspend the student from school for a period of up to one month for each offense that has been alleged by the teacher.[23]

What is remarkable about this policy is that neither the student, his parents, nor the school principal have any rights of determination or recourse, except at the end when the principal is allowed to determine the length of suspension within the limits set by the contract. Aside from this small degree of discretion, the policy clearly grants the teacher the right to dictate to both clientele and management what steps must be followed in order to receive the services of a teacher.

What is no less remarkable is that this unilateral right of determination is granted to every classroom teacher, regardless of experience, qualifications, or any other factor. Yet, anyone who has spent some time in a big-city school soon comes to recognize that there are disruptive teachers as well as disruptive students. Inexperienced teachers are especially prone to disruptive behavior. So,

too, are teachers incapable of accommodating social class and cultural differences. During the two years I spent teaching in one of Chicago's inner-city
schools, I observed nearly as many disruptive teachers as students, and of course
one disruptive teacher can create a good many disruptive students.[24] Thus,
the failure to take into account teacher culpability is almost as serious a shortcoming as the failure to make any provision for the rights of the school's clientele
and management.

All in all, the gains made by the union-rule teachers in terms of improved
working conditions are comparable to their gains in job security and salary.
The union-rule teacher is required to service fewer clients than his earlier teaching counterparts. The union-rule teacher receives far more assistance in meeting his responsibilities, and his responsibilities have been significantly reduced.
The union-rule teacher also has acquired the unprecedented right to determine which of the public school system's clientele will receive services. In
the process, of course, the rights and benefits of the schools' clientele and
management have been diminished considerably. Such is the comprehensive
and powerful nature of union rule.

Managerial and Educational Policy

So far, it can be seen that the union-rule teachers have made considerable gains,
far outdistancing their machine-rule and reform-rule counterparts along every
dimension we have examined. In turn, as the fortunes of the teachers have risen,
the fortunes of all the other school participants have declined. Most of the
policy areas in which the teachers have made gains were, as recently as a decade
ago, within the firm purview of school management and the school board. As
for the involvement and influence of the schools' clientele and the community
in school affairs, the teachers' union has extended and strengthened the barriers
surrounding the schools which were erected by the reformers. The union contract has created a closed system within another closed system. The school
clientele and local community are able to exert less influence on the schools
than ever before because school management is able to exert less influence on
the school teachers than ever before.

Indeed, it is evident and interesting that in terms of the ways the big-city
schools have been structured, the clientele and community possessed greater
ability to influence school affairs during the machine-rule period than at any
subsequent time. This is not to say, of course, that the relatively open structure
of the machine-rule school system was well exploited. It clearly was not. Nevertheless, the opportunity to do so existed, to an extent which it never has since.

Notwithstanding the remarkable gains which the teachers have made during
the union-rule period, it may be the view of some readers that the teachers
nevertheless are still not much more than "birds in a gilded cage"; they still

do not play a significant role in the general management of the big-city schools. The teachers have acquired a significant voice in the traditional areas of trade-union concern: salary and the terms and conditions of employment. However, in terms of general management, the teachers possess reactive rather than initiatory powers. They can veto, but they cannot lead.

General managerial and policy-making authority represents a critical threshold in terms of the development of union rule. We therefore shall conclude this chapter by considering three policy areas which have traditionally remained beyond the control of the industrial union: whom will the organization employ, what services will the organization provide, and how will the quality and amount of service that is provided by the organization be regulated? To oversimplify a complex matter, in the private sector these policies have remained within the control of ownership and management essentially because of the close nexus which exists between a firm's profits and its employees' benefits. No such nexus exists, however, within the public sector. Government always has lacked an adequate substitute for the profit motive. Consequently, it would appear that governments are more vulnerable than private-sector employers to demands by unions for broader forms of authority.

In his recent study of Chicago school politics, Paul Peterson concluded that the primary objective of the majority of Chicago school board members is the management of conflict.[25] Accordingly, if a teachers' union is sufficiently adamant about a given policy, and capable of buttressing its adamancy with a show of force, then there is not much reason to suppose that a school board committed to conflict management will resist for long. This would be even more the case in those policy areas where the consequences of school board capitulation will not show up as a deficit on the school board's financial records. Thus, the prospect of codetermination and even worker control over the workplace is far more likely in the public than in the private sector. There simply are far fewer constraints in the public sector.

Of course, such a prospect did not always appear likely. As table 3-3 on the school system's hiring and tenure-granting processes makes clear, the teachers only began to gain control over the workplace after they had acquired collective-bargaining rights.

In terms of the policy question, whom will the school system employ, the table indicates that during union rule the procedure for granting tenure changed in three significant ways. First, the authority to make decisions concerning tenure shifted from central to local management, namely to the school principals. This meant that instead of one central management body, the Board of Examiners, making tenure decisions, over 500 school principals would determine who was to receive tenure.

The basis upon which tenure decisions would be made also was significantly altered. When the Board of Examiners had sole tenure-granting authority, a standard written and oral examination had been administered. This meant that

Table 3-3
Standard Hiring and Tenuring Process: Chicago Public Schools, 1928-1978

Time Period	Effective Hiring Agent	Effective Tenure Agent	Compliance Mechanism	Effective Basis for Granting Tenure
1928-1946 (Machine rule)	Politicians	Politicians	Political sponsorship	Political accommodation
1947-1966 (Reform rule)	Central school management	Central school management	Central Board of Examiners	Passage of standard written/oral exam
1967-1978 (Union rule)	Central school management	Local school management	Union-Board contract	Approval of local principal after 3 years of teaching

Sources: Data for the machine-rule and reform-rule periods are drawn from Mary Herrick, *The Chicago Schools: A Social and Political History* (Beverly Hills, Cal.: Sage Publications, 1971). Sources for the union-rule period are the *Proceedings of the Chicago Board of Education* and the *Agreements between the Chicago School Board and the Chicago Teachers' Union.*

all of the teachers in the system possessed a more or less common body of knowledge and level of skills. The school principals, on the other hand, make their assessment of a teacher's competence on a basis of how well a teacher performs in the classroom. While the change to a performance-based assessment has much merit in principle, in practice the change virtually assures that educational knowledge and skills will frequently no longer be used as significant criteria for the award of tenure.

The outcome obtains for two primary reasons. First, achieving order tends to take precedence over teaching in a large number of big-city schools. This is because order is often a serious problem and because expectations about student abilities to learn often are lower. It is, of course, predominantly in the inner-city schools that one finds these twin problems. The inner-city schools also happen to be where the majority of the school system's newer teachers are located, and, hence, where most of the tenure decisions are made.[26]

The other factor favoring the use of classroom-management skills over educational skills is that from a school principal's point of view, it is a straightforward matter to assess classroom order, whereas determining a teacher's educational skills is a far more complex and controversial matter. It also is in a school principal's interest to place a good deal of regard on classroom management where disorder is more of a problem. Consequently, a large number of teachers who would not have been able to achieve tenure during reform rule because of deficiencies in educational knowledge and skills regularly receive tenure because of the union-rule criteria.

The third significant change which occurs during union rule is the use of the union–board contract as the source of authority concerning the tenure-awarding process. Certain contract stipulations virtually assure that very few teachers will be denied tenure, regardless of the level of their educational or classroom-management skills. The contract accomplishes this radical change in two ways. It states that in order to acquire tenure, a teacher need only perform at a "satisfactory" level. As satisfactory is defined, it is the lowest of three possible positive ratings which a principal may assign to a teacher's performance. Thus, a principal is directed to award tenure to teachers who are performing at only the minimal level of competency.[27]

The other contract stipulation we discussed earlier. In order to assign a rating of "unsatisfactory," a principal must observe an elaborate and time-consuming procedure of notification, well-documented justification, the involvement of higher school officials, and so forth. Given the ambiguity of educational-performance criteria and the minimal competency criteria called for by the contract, building a case for an unsatisfactory performance is no simple task. Undoubtedly, a good number of principals decline to make the investment of time and effort that is required. Consequently, some teachers acquire tenure even though they possess very few teaching or classroom-management skills.

Another important policy question involves the determination of who decides what services will be provided by the school system. To the limited extent that this policy has been studied, two general conclusions usually have been reached with regard to the role of the teachers' union. The union is a conservative force in school affairs, favoring a status quo position on most matters of policy and practice. However, the teachers' union has focused its attention almost exclusively on salary and related concerns, displaying only limited interest in the areas of educational services and policies.[28]

Based upon the evidence we have examined so far, the first conclusion does not take into sufficient regard the genuinely radical changes entailed by union rule. Union rule differs fundamentally from any preceding purpose and form of school governance. The teachers' union seeks and is acquiring in a number of respects a unique, autonomous status for the teachers within the big-city school system. What an autonomous status entails is that teachers no longer will be bound by the dictates and discretionary actions of school management, nor will the needs of the school system's clientele and the local community be significant factors in determining a course of action for the teachers, except as those needs are defined by the teachers. Union rule intends and is transforming the big-city public schools so that they serve principally the interests of teachers, as those interests are determined by the teachers' union.

A remarkable incident reported in a study of school policy exemplifies the singularly far-reaching impact of union rule and the radical difference between union rule and the preceding forms of educational governance. As the story is told, a school principal called a staff meeting, which ran over the time allotted by the union contract for such events. One teacher therefore left the meeting prior to its conclusion and subsequently filed a grievance concerning the meeting's excessive length.

Inasmuch as the principal indeed had violated the contract by allowing the meeting to run too long, the hearing officer of course ruled in favor of the grieving teacher. However, thirty-eight other teachers in attendance at the meeting sent a signed petition to the union in which they expressed dissatisfaction with the unilateral action of the grievant and strong support for the principal, whom they described as an "exemplary supervisor and sincere friend." The union responded by pointing to one of union rule's most distinguishing characteristics.

> The [organization] takes the view that such a statement is irrelevant and immaterial since neither the proficiency of the principal as a supervisor nor his personal or professional relations with staff members has any bearing on whether [he] has violated the by-law as alleged in the [grievant's] appeal. . . . We urge the teachers signing the petition to distinguish between principals and principles."[29]

This mundane incident clarifies three critical aspects of union rule involving school governance and service delivery. The locus of authority for school policy formation and service delivery shifts under union rule. Union rule places authority within the contract, rather than with the discretion of teachers, management, or the school board. In turn, the nature of authority is altered by union rule. Managerial prerogatives, teacher discretion, client needs, and community preferences become residual considerations and bases for action, falling within the increasingly diminishing interstices of union rule. Finally, the purpose of authority and the services to be delivered by the school system are changed by union rule. The intent of the contract from the union's point of view is to maximize and guarantee the rights and benefits of the school system's teachers. To the extent the union is successful, the services and benefits received by the school system's clientele and the public become in effect the by-products of a system geared principally to serving teachers' interests.

As for the limited interest which is said to be shown by the teachers' union in the general management of the schools, particularly in the so-called educational-policy areas, the problem with such an interpretation lies mainly with a failure to appreciate the political constraints under which a union's leadership must operate. Just as in electoral politics outside the school system, the union leadership periodically must stand for election. In order to succeed electorally, the leadership perforce emulates the strategies and tactics of the politicians. The union leadership emphasizes the concrete and noncontroversial benefits it delivers to the general membership, which principally are salary increases and class-size reductions.

However, an examination of the teacher union–school board contract reveals that the teachers' union also engages in two other types of activity. The union delivers substantial benefits to a wide range of subgroups within the union's membership. Thus, approximately 40 percent of the articles in the Chicago teacher union's contract pertain to specific subgroups within the bargaining unit, such as physical education teachers, teacher aides, librarians, and so forth. These efforts are, of course, not given as much publicity as efforts toward securing general benefits. To do so would be to foster competition among the subgroups and thereby impair the sense of unity the union leadership strives to achieve.

Additionally, the union leadership engages in a number of ongoing activities, which in part benefit particular subgroups, but which more generally involve controlling the environment within which the union must operate. The contract points up any number of such activities, and a good number of them involve the general management of the schools, while others display the union's interest in many so-called educational-policy areas.

Thus, in addition to the annual contract negotiating session between the union and the board, the contract provides for a regular series of monthly meetings between the union's leadership and the superintendent of the schools. This of course provides the union leadership with an ongoing opportunity for managerial input on a wide range of issues. A similar series of regular monthly meetings is called for at the local school level. At each of the city's schools, the school principal is required to meet with the union's "Professional Problems Committee," which is made up of union-affiliated teachers from the local school. So, here too a number of policies and practices come up for joint determination.

In terms of specific educational policy, each annual contract calls for a broad range of joint teacher union–school board committees. The committees have covered virtually every type of educational program policy There have been committees on bilingual and bicultural education programs; specific types of curricular offerings, such as the high school social studies program; and innovative programs for the inner-city schools, to mention just a few examples.[30]

Thus, given all these opportunities to participate in the deliberations of the school board, the general superintendent, and local school management, if the teachers' union is not performing as a comanager of the schools and formulating a wide variety of educational policies, then the union's representatives to these meetings and committees are highly ineffectual negotiators. At the same time, however, the union should not be expected to emphasize its participation as a comanager of the schools or to take public positions on many of the policies it has helped to formulate. Many policies in these areas are controversial and productive of divisiveness. In those instances where the union has gone public with an educational program, the program typically has amounted to a variation on the theme of "more is better," such as service-saturation programs for improving the inner-city schools. Such programs translate into more jobs and salaries, of course, and therefore would not be regarded as controversial innovations by most union members.

The final policy question we shall consider concerns the amount and the quality of service which is provided by the school system. We already have discussed both to some extent. We learned, for instance, that the amount of service provided by a given classroom teacher has declined significantly under union rule. This change has been accomplished by the frequent reductions in class size which the teachers' union has been able to negotiate. We also saw that under union rule teachers have secured the right to withhold their services from any clients who are unwilling to conform to the behavioral standards set by a given teacher. Finally, the quality of school services has declined under union rule. Because of changes in the tenure-granting procedure and the difficulties associated with the assignment of an "unsatisfactory" rating to a teacher's performance, most teachers who gain entry to the school system also will gain tenure, regardless of the level of their teaching abilities.

In addition to these reductions in the amount and quality of service, union rule also has had a racially discriminatory effect on the amount and quality of service which is being provided by the school system. Some sections of the city receive more and better services than others, and the sections which receive fewer and poorer services are overwhelmingly black.

However, in order to properly appreciate union rule, it is important to recognize that racial discrimination in the distribution of services is not an objective of the teachers' union. It is an outcome of union rule. The objective of the union, as we have said, is to transform and then maintain the school system so that it principally serves the interests of the teachers. If in accomplishing its objective the interests of other school participants are poorly served, then that is simply a problem which is beyond the scope of the union's consideration and concern.

Thus, it happened that by steadfastly protecting two traditional teacher benefits, voluntary transfer and transfer preference on the basis of seniority, the teachers' union has become responsible for the assignment of three unique functions to the school system's inner-city schools. The inner-city schools are in effect assigned the responsibility of serving as the primary induction center for new teachers entering the school system. In turn, the inner-city schools are therefore required to function as the school system's primary training center for inexperienced teachers. Then, since most new teachers begin teaching in the inner-city schools and because poorly qualified teachers find it difficult to transfer to other schools, the inner-city schools function as the main repository for the school system's most poorly qualified teachers.[31]

The steadfastness with which the teachers' union has fought to maintain the teacher benefits in question is attested to by the loss of several million dollars in federal aid. The loss has occurred because the federal government has withheld disbursement of funds to the Chicago school system until the effects of its discriminatory practices are removed. In spite of the loss in federal aid, the union has resisted altering the teachers' benefit policies of voluntary transfer and seniority preference in assignment, which are responsible for the discriminatory effects that the federal government objects to.

The way the two policies operate is that in December and June of each school year vacancies are announced, with the list of vacancies including those positions held by nontenured teachers. As a result of this procedure, three distinct teacher-transfer patterns occur. Tenured teachers move into any vacancy on the list, including positions held by the nontenured teachers, since preference is given to seniority. After the senior teachers have moved, the nontenured teachers move into those vacancies which have not been occupied by the seniors. Finally, the teachers entering the school system at the beginning of the following term are put into a position of having to choose among the leftovers.[32]

The outcome is virtually a three-ring school system. The system's tenured senior teachers teach in an outer ring of schools for the most part. Mainly, these schools are located along the city's outlying areas, and they serve the city's middle-class children. Tenured teachers with less seniority and a number of nontenured teachers, depending upon their proportion in the system, teach within a middle ring of schools. Located between the city's outskirts and the inner city, these schools service mainly a working-class clientele. The school system's recruits, as well as the teachers who find it difficult to move because of limited qualifications, are therefore confined to the inner ring of schools. The inner ring is of course located in the inner city, and the clientele of the inner-city schools is made up of the city's poor.

Consequently, the inner-city schools are distinguished by three unique characteristics. Inner-city school teachers possess the least experience in teaching. The inner-city schools experience the highest levels of teacher transiency, because as teachers gain seniority they acquire the ability to move from their original place of assignment. The inner-city schools also have the largest number of poorly qualified teachers, because those teachers lacking in skills find it more difficult to find a school principal who is willing to approve their transfer.

Since of the three functions, serving as a repository for poorly qualified teachers clearly has the most pronounced negative effect, it may be worthwhile to conclude by considering the reason why the teachers' union apparently has elected not to eliminate the principals' discretionary rights in the acceptance of incoming teachers to their schools. Leaving principals with the right to deny entry to certain teachers would certainly seem to constitute a clear case of infringement on the voluntary and seniority-based rights of teacher transfer. In view of the many areas of management discretion which the teachers' union has been able to eliminate, it would seem a relatively simple matter to negotiate the elimination of this particular problem area.

There appear to be two main reasons why school principals have been allowed to retain discretion in this regard despite the establishment of union rule, which is so fundamentally geared to teacher benefits and protection. It is, to begin with, in the interest of the teachers' union as well as the school board to confine the system's least competent teachers to the inner-city schools. In the inner city the amount of parental involvement in the schools is lower, the efficacy of the limited amount of parental involvement which does exist is lower as well, and the clientele conventionally is regarded as less educable. The mutual interest of the union and the board in taking advantage of the inner-city school characteristics rests upon their desire to present the school system in a favorable manner. If teachers were allowed to freely distribute themselves throughout the school system, the poorly qualified teachers would be more noticeable and objections to their presence in the system more likely would be raised by middle-class parents. Thus, the inner city represents the best and indeed an excellent haven for harboring the system's incompetent teachers.[33]

The second reason is that just as it is in the interest of the school board and the teachers' union to maintain poorly qualified teachers in the inner-city schools, it is in the interest of poorly qualified teachers to remain in the inner city. Much has been written about the difficulties of teaching in the inner city. However, a good many teachers do not subscribe to this point of view. The inner-city schools represent the low-demand and low-expectation sector of the school system for teachers as well as students. Therefore, teachers who possess a limited interest in teaching or who are incapable of effective teaching find the inner-city schools well suited to their needs. Lack of progress plausibly can be attributed to the low quality of the clientele.

In turn, there certainly is little reason to expect that the teachers' union would elect to discriminate against the interests of this particular group of teachers. The union is committed to the interests of all members of the bargaining unit, the least worthy as well as the most worthy.

Notes

1. Harold Lasswell, *Politics: Who Gets What, When, How* (Cleveland: Meridian Books, 1958. Originally published by McGraw-Hill, 1936), pp. 13, 113.

2. A discussion of this shortcoming is provided by Robert Lineberry, *Equality and Urban Policy: The Distribution of Municipal Public Services* (Beverly Hills, Cal.: Sage Publications, 1977).

3. See chapter 1, note 12.

4. See chapter 2, note 6.

5. Comprehensive bibliographies have been compiled by Frederick M. Wirt and Paul E. Peterson. Wirt's is contained in Michael W. Kirst, ed., *State, School, and Politics: Research Directions* (Lexington, Mass.: Lexington Books, D.C. Heath, 1972). Peterson's is in his "The Politics of American Education," manuscript in preparation.

6. Wesley Wildman and Fred Lifton, *Collective Bargaining Contract Analyzer* (Springfield, Ill.: Illinois School Board Association, 1975). As this publication indicates, school boards also are beginning to develop centralized and standardized strategies in an effort to more effectively negotiate with the unions.

7. Paul E. Peterson, *School Politics: Chicago Style* (Chicago: University of Chicago Press, 1976), p. 198.

8. Barry Shapiro, *The Chicago Teachers' Union and The Ghetto* (M.S. thesis, Department of Political Science, University of Chicago, 1968). Cited in Peterson, *School Politics*, p. 197.

9. Wildman and Lifton, *Contract Analyzer*, p. 6.

10. The union frequently does not negotiate the same salary increases across all pay grades. Accordingly, in figure 3-1 "average" salaries were constructed by taking a figure midway between minimum and maximum salaries for teachers with the B.A. degree. Where salary increases for "longevity" were provided, these increases were excluded in order to keep the time period between minimum and maximum salary attainment approximately equal. Where different salary schedules were used for elementary and high school teachers, the two figures were combined and the midpoint was used.

11. Mary J. Herrick, *The Chicago Schools: A Social and Political History* (Beverly Hills, Cal.: Sage Publications, 1971).

12. *Facts and Figures: The Chicago Public Schools* (Chicago: Board of Education) for the respective years is the data source for the reform-rule period. The Board of Education ceased publication of this informative annual pamphlet in 1971, claiming that compiling and publishing costs had become prohibitive.

13. The source for the benefits under union rule is the *Agreement between the Chicago Board of Education and the Chicago Teachers' Union* for the years in question. The fringe benefit appropriation is contained in *Highlights and Perspectives: 1975-76 Tentative Budget* (Chicago: Board of Education), p. 78.

14. In 1976 the policy was further amended so that a surviving spouse could collect the benefits, thus further transforming the policy into a form of life insurance. *Board-Union Agreement*, article 37, 1976.

15. Raymond Callahan provides a useful discussion of performance accountability, particularly for the early reform period. See *Education and the Cult of Efficiency* (Chicago: University of Chicago Press, 1962).

16. James S. Coleman and his associates analyzed most of the presumably effective factors and found them to be largely insignificant. James S. Coleman, et al., *Equality of Educational Opportunity* (Washington, D.C.: Office of Education, 1966).

17. *Board–Union Agreement*, article 39. A provision in the first contract between the board and the union stipulated that a joint board–union committee would develop the evaluation procedure.

18. Interview conducted by the author as a member of the Illinois Governor's Task Force on School Finance, October 1975.

19. In my capacity as interviewer for the Governor's Task Force, several school principals, officials of the Principals' Association, and officials of the Assistant Principals' Association informed me that collective bargaining has had a demoralizing effect on local school management. Local managers have no input into the negotiations, yet the burden of implementing the contract falls heavily on them, and central management provides little support or interpretation of the contract terms. Consequently, many school principals exercise very little authority for fear of overstepping bounds which may or may not exist in the contract.

20. Herrick, *Chicago Schools*, p. 181, provided the 1920s data, and *Facts and Figures* contains data for the reform-rule period.

21. *Report of the Governor's Task Force on School Finance* (Springfield, Ill.: Office of the Governor, 1975), p. viii.

22. Teacher aides became a part of the bargaining unit in 1971. Consequently, the union has a self-interest in having additional aides hired.

23. *Board–Union Agreement*, article 30.

24. It was highly unusual to observe disruption in an experienced teacher's classes. The few experienced teachers who did encounter disruptions made little effort to hide their dislike for the students; undoubtedly the students sensed the teacher's attitude and this at least in part contributed to the disruption.

25. Peterson, *School Politics*, p. 191.

26. The procedure whereby the bulk of new teachers is placed in inner-city schools is discussed in greater detail shortly.

27. The ratings a principal may assign to a teacher's performance are "superior," "excellent," "satisfactory," and "unsatisfactory." Because of the difficulties surrounding the assignment of an unsatisfactory rating, a rating of "satisfactory" may well indicate an unsatisfactory performance.

28. This view is the prevailing one among political scientists and others who have studied public employee unions, but other researchers find alternative interpretations more satisfactory. See chapter 1, note 4.

29. Charles R. Perry and Wesley A. Wildman, *The Impact of Negotiations in Public Education: The Evidence from the Schools* (Worthington, Ohio: Charles A. Jones Publishing Co., 1970), pp. 202–203.

30. *Board–Union Agreement,* article 1, article 44. Article 1 contains a general statement on the principle of codetermination. Article 44 covers the various topics encompassed by the joint board–union committees.

31. The union certainly did not create these functions for the inner-city schools. In 1951 the sociologist Howard Becker described the functions in a doctoral dissertation, *Role and Career Problems of the Chicago Public Schools Teachers* (Ph.D. dissertation, University of Chicago, 1951).

32. In the 1976 *Board–Union Agreement,* the standard transfer procedure was placed in abeyance for three years for the purpose of complying with a long-standing request from HEW that the faculty of the city's schools be racially integrated. New teachers are being assigned in a manner that enhances integration. This integration-by-attrition policy is the product of many years of negotiation among the union, the board, and HEW.

33. There are, of course, some excellent teachers who prefer to teach in the inner-city schools. However, the ethos of the several inner-city schools in which I taught was resignation and indifference. Dedicated teachers are considered odd by many of their colleagues, and this ethos drives many excellent teachers from the inner-city schools in search of a more congenial and supportive group of colleagues.

4

The Political Basis
for Union Rule

Introduction

In the preceding chapter our attention was focused upon a major big-city public bureaucracy, the Chicago public schools. This was done in order to describe some of union rule's critical and distinguishing characteristics and to determine the extent to which union rule has developed in the schools. The method used to make the analysis was to compare "who got what" from the schools under three distinct forms of governance. Under the union-rule form of governance the teachers acquired unprecedented political as well as economic benefits. At the same time, the traditional elites of big-city school politics, the politicians under machine rule and the school administrators under reform rule, both incurred substantial losses as a result of union rule. Thus, we concluded that a revolution was occurring in big-city politics, with the teachers having emerged as a new elite.

It remains to account for the basis of the revolution. Our attention in this chapter, then, shall be upon "who got what when": under what circumstances did union rule emerge and then further develop in the big-city bureaucracy that we have examined? Accordingly, we must now extend our focus beyond the big-city bureaucracy to encompass big-city politics as well.

Two general phenomena were discussed in chapter 2 as accounting for the rise of union rule. The declining strength of the big-city political organization has made it more vulnerable to the demands of organized public employees. Edward Banfield and James Q. Wilson have described the relationship between the political party and organized public bureaucrats in terms of a continuum. "Where party organization is strong, the city administration is in a relatively good position to resist the demands of the organized employees."[1]

The other phenomenon is the altered organizational strength of organized labor. As the economy shifted from a labor to a service base, organized labor's traditional source of membership in turn diminished. As a result, during the 1960s organized labor began to make a concerted effort to organize employees in the burgeoning service sector, particularly government employees. Then, as the proportion of public employees within organized labor increased, the public union leaders acquired an increasingly influential leadership role within the AFL-CIO authority structure.[2] The twin phenomena resulted in the establishment of varying degrees of union rule in the big cities during the 1960s and on into the 1970s.

A model constructed by Theodore Lowi focuses upon the modern relationship among the politicians, organized labor, and city employees.[3] Lowi's model basically consists of three stages. The first two stages generally resemble the relationships encompassed by our machine- and reform-rule forms of government. Using data mainly from the 1961 New York City mayoral election, Lowi then goes on to describe a radical development, which constitutes the beginning of a third major state.

During this stage, having lost virtually all organizational strength, the politicians bring the reform-rule leadership (consisting of bureau commissioners and so forth) and the union-rule leadership (the heads of the larger public unions) into a full partnership for the purpose of winning reelection. According to Lowi, "Before the end of the [1961] election most of the larger city bureaucracies had political representation in the inner core of the new Administration."[4]

For our purposes, Lowi's model is deficient in three important respects. To begin, the third stage applies only to those big cities whose political leadership is so bereft of wit and strength that it brings the formal and informal leadership of the public bureaucracies into full partnership. Presumably, however, in cities possessed of a political leadership which is more prudent and less politically eviscerated than that of New York City's, some lesser forms of alliance would be formed before complete capitulation occurs.

A more critical shortcoming is that Lowi's modeling ends just at the point where most of the interesting developments are likely to begin to occur. Having put together into a leadership alliance three such distinct and dynamic forms of leadership, which we would term machine, reform and union rule, Lowi leaves it at that. He does suggest, by terming the political consequences of the alliance "the bureaucratic state," that the reform-rule leadership comes out on top in the triumvirate. Yet, such an outcome has not been confirmed by subsequent events in New York City or elsewhere, and, in any event, the outcome is not sufficiently described by Lowi.

The final deficiency is that Lowi contends his model bears no relationship to developments in Chicago. Chicago, he says, is unique because of its political machine and therefore unrepresentative of politics elsewhere. While it is true that Chicago's politics do not fit the particular pattern of events described by Lowi, much of the logic contained in Lowi's model nevertheless does apply to all big-city politics of the 1960s and 1970s, including Chicago's. This is certainly the case in the phenomena we are examining, school politics.

The model presented here overcomes the principal deficiencies in Lowi's model, and it complies with what we have described as the twin developments leading to the establishment of union rule. As the organizational strength of the politicians has waned, the organizational strength of the unionized public employees has waxed. Thus, in the struggle for benefits, the public unions have been able to make unprecedented gains.

Who Gets What When

The first task of this chapter is to demonstrate a decline in the strength of the Chicago political organization. The decline must of course be of a sufficient magnitude to make a compelling case for the organization's diminished ability to resist the demands of the organized school teachers. This may be considered as the vulnerability factor. In assessing the strength of the Chicago political organization, it is important to recognize that it need not match the low ebb of, say, New York City's political parties before it reaches a state of vulnerability. Thus, while we do demonstrate a significant decline in the Chicago political organization's strength, we decidedly are not saying that the so-called machine has reached a state of demise. Rather, it is shown that the political organization currently operates with a significantly altered, less durable, and weakened basis of organizational strength.

The second task of the chapter is to demonstrate that the diminishment of the political organization's strength corresponds to the emergence and development of union rule in the schools. As we learned in chapter 2, union rule developed essentially in two stages. A modified form of union rule existed between 1966 and 1972; then in 1973 a more fully developed form emerged. Of course, the progression that occurred in Chicago is not inevitable. The extent of union rule's development depends largely upon the degree to which the union is operated in an independent and self-interested fashion. Therefore, if the political side of the relationship represents a vulnerability factor, the union side may be said to represent an attack factor.

Union rule emerged slowly in Chicago because the union leadership initially elected to moderate its demands in deference to the politicians' preferences. However, as we saw, the union leadership's moderate course of action ultimately led to its demise at the hands of a leadership group committed to achieving a more fully developed form of union rule. Of the two forms we examined, the more fully developed form of union rule clearly represents a more stable form. In contrast to the moderate leadership, the militant leadership is not opposed by any significant elements within the union. It may be said, therefore, that attack, rather than accommodation, represents the equilibrium point of union rule.

The method of examination that will be employed requires that we look more closely than we have so far at the Chicago political organization under the leadership of Mayor Richard Daley. For it was in 1966, at the midpoint of Daley's term (1955–1976), that union rule first emerged in the schools. Union rule subsequently developed more fully during the remainder of Daley's term as mayor and thereafter. Thus, it can be seen that the term of the Daley political organization spanned three distinct phases of union rule's development.[5]

It can be documented with electoral data that the strength of the Chicago political organization has undergone three distinct phases, corresponding to the three phases of union rule. That is, it is possible to distinguish three forms of political organization possessing declining degrees of strength during the years of Mayor Daley's leadership and thereafter, and these political phases correspond with the phases of union rule's development.

From 1955 to 1965, the Daley political organization functioned closely after the manner of a classic political machine, and during this time it operated at the zenith of its strength. These are, of course, the years prior to the development of union rule in the schools. Then, in 1966 the classic political machine entered a period of partial disintegration, and its organizational strength showed signs of diminishment. Correspondingly, 1966 marks the year that the school board, at the politicians' insistence, agreed to grant the teachers collective bargaining. Finally, by the 1970s the Chicago political organization no longer bears the characteristics of a classic political machine, and its organizational strength has declined to an unprecedented low level. It was, at the same time, during the 1970s that union rule in the schools emerged in fully developed form. Thus, the correspondence between the two developments is striking. We shall therefore look in greater detail at each of the developments.

The Classic Inner-City Machine: 1955–1965

The Chicago Democratic political organization is by all accounts the most powerful big-city political party in the nation. Yet just as with any political organization, the Chicago party is no monolith. It has its primary base of support; secondary bases of support, which are less reliable and electorally significant; and in some areas of the city, the party has very little support at all.

What distinguishes the Chicago organization from all other big-city political organizations is the extent to which it has been able to maintain a monopoly of control in two critical political areas: in the inner city during all elections and in the entire city during primary elections. It is in fact just such a twin monopoly which has been said to distinguish the political machine from other less powerful forms of political organization.[6]

There is a third factor, emphasized more by political candidates than political scientists, which distinguishes a political machine: vote size. Machines turn out larger votes than other forms of political organization typically do. Thus, it has been maintained that the Chicago political organization enters citywide elections with a built-in margin of approximately 200,000 votes.[7] This principally is a result of the size of the party's patronage system of public employment. The effectiveness of the party's precinct operation, manned by the patronage employees, also lends significantly to the party's initial advantage. Of course, vote size is to a large extent a function of the control the political party possesses in the inner city and to a lesser extent elsewhere. Nevertheless, size is analytically and substantively distinct from control.

In an interesting study of the Daley political organization, a politically well-connected and experienced local news commentator, Len O'Connor, quite accurately identified one of the machine's classic monopolies.[8] O'Connor characterized a group of Chicago's inner-city wards as the "automatic eleven." The wards were so designated because they produced with remarkable regularity massive pluralities for candidates slated for office by the machine. Regardless of the office being contested, issues raised, quality of the opposition, or anything else for that matter, the eleven wards always produced enormous pluralities.

O'Connor reinforces his point by recounting the political consequences of a gruesome gangland-style slaying of an alderman from one of the machine's automatic-eleven wards. The slaying occurred just after a primary election, and hence speculation was raised that the event would negatively affect the general election vote. Presumably, at least the faint-hearted and the personal followers of the alderman might be expected to stay home. Yet the vote in that election turned out to be indistinguishable from any other vote: huge and Democratic.[9] Such is the indifference which distinguishes a genuinely controlled machine vote.

The method employed here to confirm the existence of monopoly control in the inner-city wards is to analyze electoral data for the election which from the political organization's point of view is the most critical: the mayoral general election. While this placement of value generally would hold true for any big-city political organization, in Chicago there is no question as to the paramount importance of the mayoral general election. For Richard Daley was not only the mayoral candidate, Daley also was the all-powerful head of the political organization. Consequently, when a precinct worker failed to deliver in this particular election, it was not for lack of effort or incentive. Under a patronage system of employment, job security is intimately connected to precinct performance.

Listed in table 4-1 are the top fifteen wards in the city in terms of plurality production for Mayor Daley during Daley's first three mayoral general elections, occurring in 1955, 1959, and 1963. Accompanying the rank ordering is a Chicago ward map (figure 4-1) which indicates where the Daley political organization's primary base of support was located during these elections.

What the data reveal is that during this period the Chicago political organization possessed to a remarkable degree one of the primary characteristics of a classic political machine. Each one of the top fifteen wards for Daley is located in the inner city, forming one huge and contiguous mass of primary support. Since it becomes significant at a later point, it should be mentioned that all of the city's black wards are represented in the top-fifteen listing. In general during this time period, the city's politics can best be characterized as inner-city Democrats versus outer-city Republicans.

O'Connor inexplicably left two critically important wards off his "automatic eleven" listing, the Eleventh and the Twenty-fifth. The Eleventh Ward is none other than Mayor Daley's home ward, and as might be expected, it invariably ranks at the top or very near the top in every election. Since patronage plays

Table 4–1
**The Classic Inner-City Machine, 1955–1963: Daley's Top Fifteen Plurality-
Producing Wards**

Rank	Ward	Member of O'Connor's "Automatic Eleven"
1	24	
2	11	no
3	29	
4	2	
5	3	
6	1	
7	27	
8	20	
9	25	no
10	4	
11	31	
12	26	no
13	14	no
14	6	
15	16	no

Source: Chicago Board of Election Commissioners.

an important role in turning out a sizable vote, the performance of the Eleventh
Ward is not surprising. Knowledgeable observers have estimated the number of
patronage jobs held by Daley's Eleventh-Ward neighbors as 20–25 percent of the
city's entire patronage pool. As for the Twenty-fifth Ward, while it is no match
for Daley's Eleventh either in terms of performance or patronage, it nevertheless
never fell below the eleventh position during any mayoral elections between
1955 and 1977.

Our listing, on the other hand, leaves off one of O'Connor's "automatic eleven" wards, the Twenty-eighth. The Twenty-eighth Ward is a good example of the
distinction between vote control and vote size. In the parlance of Chicago politics,
the Twenty-eighth Ward is a producer of the pure product: nearly every vote cast
in the ward is a Democratic vote. However, not a great many votes are cast. Therefore, in terms of our plurality criteria, the Twenty-eighth Ward does not produce
enough of the pure product to qualify among even our fifteen-ward listing.

The second characteristic of a classic machine is monopoly control over
primary elections throughout the entire city. David Greenstone and Paul Peterson have analyzed this type of electoral data for a portion of the time period
under consideration here.[10] They analyzed Chicago Democratic primary elections for state representative for the years 1958 to 1964, which cover four
elections. The results of their analysis amply justify characterizing the Chicago
political organization as a machine during this time.

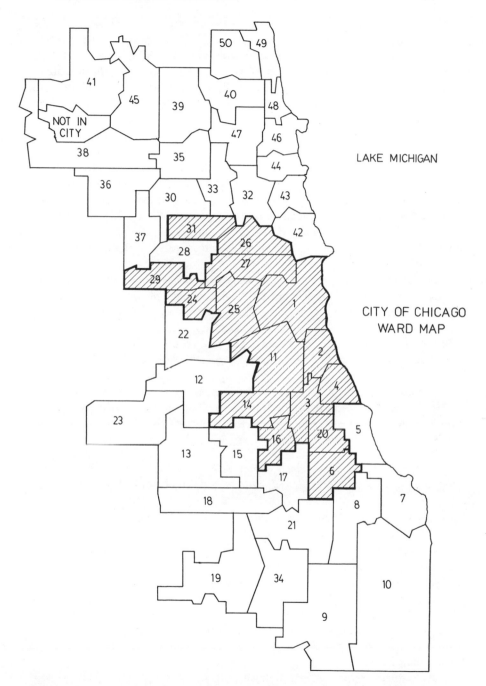

Figure 4-1. The Classic Inner-City Machine's Primary Base of Support, 1955–1963

Greenstone and Peterson found that in nearly 80 percent of the Democratic state representative primaries, the candidates slated for office by the machine were not even contested. Thus, endorsement by the machine was a virtual guarantee of election. Moreover, in those few elections where the machine's candidates were opposed, the opposition did not represent much of a threat. Only 8 percent of the challengers managed to get as much as 20 percent of the vote, and in no instance did a challenger's vote exceed 39 percent. Thus, the data are awesome evidence indeed of the strength of the Chicago political organization. Its monopoly over the office of state representative was absolute.

In the third area we are examining for evidence of the existence of a classic machine, vote size, once again the Chicago political organization's achievements are of classic proportions. The Daley political organization produced its two largest presidential election votes during the years 1955 to 1965. In 1960 the Chicago vote for John Kennedy tipped the 1-million mark. Four years later, the political organization turned out an even larger vote for Lyndon Johnson: 1,141,148.[11]

In the mayoral general elections, Daley faced his two most difficult challenges during this period, and the political organization did very well on his behalf. Against Robert Merriam in 1955, Daley received over 700,000 votes, and in 1963 when he was opposed by Benjamin Adamowski, Daley received 679,497. In 1959, a year the Republicans put up only a token challenge, the vote produced by the political organization was a phenomenal 778,612.

Thus, in all three respects, inner-city control, primary election control, and vote productivity, the Chicago political organization functioned as a classic political machine during the period 1955 to 1965. Rarely challenged and less rarely beaten, the organization was at the zenith of its strength during these years.

School Politics during the Classic Machine Period: 1955–1965

In order for Richard Daley to win his first mayoral election, the political organization had to defeat two candidates with substantial backing among the city's business and reform interests. In the 1955 primary, Daley faced Martin Kennelly, the two-term incumbent mayor that the machine had dumped in order to slate Daley. Prior to becoming mayor, Kennelly had been a successful businessman and a prominent civic leader. In the general election, Daley was opposed by Robert Merriam, who turned out to be the candidate with the broadest base of appeal the Republicans ever managed to field against Daley. In addition to Republicans, Merriam received support from independent Democrats and liberals in general.

Accordingly, upon winning, Daley's central task was clear: he had to coopt the business and reform interests that had opposed his candidacy. As far as our analysis is concerned, this meant that the political organization definitely had to keep politics out of the schools. Thus, Daley became an ardent advocate of reform rule in the schools.[12]

After all, under Mayor Daley's predecessor, Kennelly, the schools finally had been pulled out of the pits of disrespectability into which years of machine abuse had sunk them. What Kennelly of course had done was to hire prominent reform superintendents from out of town and then give them a free hand in directing the schools. Therefore, by carrying on the Kennelly tradition, some of Kennelly's reform image would very likely rub off on Daley. Whereas, if Daley involved himself in the schools in any way, cries undoubtedly would arise that he was reverting to the terrible ways of the Kelly–Nash administration.

Another major reason for keeping politics out of the schools was that Daley had inherited a school superintendent, Benjamin Willis, who adamantly opposed lay influence on school decision making. Willis's opposition extended even to school board members, and therefore it definitely included politicians. Given Willis's solid backing among professional educators and, even more importantly, the city's businessmen, the stakes would have had to be high indeed in order to induce Daley to assault Willis's formidable reform fortress.

However, the stakes were not at all high. For Daley also had inherited a school system that had been effectively dismantled as a significant patronage and spoils enterprise. Therefore, during the early years of Daley's administration the political organization was content to allow the schools to operate independently of the city's politics.

As for the teachers, because of the separation between the schools and politics which had occurred in 1947, by 1955 the teachers' interests had turned mainly inward upon the schools. After a highly auspicious beginning in 1937 as the first united and the most militant teachers' union in the nation, the leadership of the Chicago Teachers' Union had mellowed. With the withdrawal of the great external enemy (the politicians) from the schools, the union entered into a period of what may be called organizational drift. This is attested to by the small growth in the union's membership. In 1940, the membership was 8,171; fifteen years later it had increased to only 8,618.[13]

The strategy that the union leadership pursued in order to acquire benefit increases was to form a close alliance with the reform management of the schools. Given the strong anti-machine behavior which the teachers' union had displayed during the 1940s and the disinclination of the politicians to intervene in school affairs, the union leadership actually did not have much of an alternative but to ally itself with management. Nevertheless, as we saw in chapter 3, the union leadership's strategy paid off handsomely. The teachers acquired unprecedented gains from both Superintendents Hunt and Willis.[14]

Two major events in the early 1960s, however, upset the comfortable relations between the politicians and school managers and the school managers and teachers. The schools became the center of an enormous civil-rights controversy that finally began to spill over into the city's politics. Further away from the city, but no less significant in terms of political impact, public employees began to acquire collective-bargaining rights, notably the New York City teachers. As a result, many of Chicago's teachers began to find the union leadership's informal negotiations with school management an unacceptable means of acquiring benefits. Both events, as we shall see, had significant political consequences.

The Classic Machine in Transition: 1966–1969

Forms of political organization and government typically change slowly, except occasionally during times of large-scale revolution. Even during revolutions, the changes which occur in political and governmental form may not be accompanied by much significant change in the distribution of benefits. As the saying goes, the conductors change but the music remains the same.

The changes in political organization which occurred in Chicago between 1966 and 1969 are far from revolutionary. However, what the changes lack in immediate significance is made up for by the portent they possess of similar and much greater changes to come. The die was cast during this period, so to speak. For this reason, the brief period under consideration here is characterized as transitional. The political organization in its classic form begins to disintegrate; however, it remains basically intact and possessed of formidable strength.

To better appreciate the significance of the changes occurring during this period, it is useful to take into account the mayoral general election of 1963. This election pitted Daley against one of only two significant challengers he ever had to confront, Benjamin Adamowski. Adamowski possessed a number of qualities that are highly valued in Chicago politics. He was Polish, in a city with an enormous Polish and Eastern European population. He had a background as a "law-and-order" type of states attorney. Finally, he was a Democrat, only thinly disguised as a Republican in order to make the general election challenge against Daley.[15]

What is significant about Adamowski's challenge are the sources of his strength and his weakness as a candidate. Adamowski cut heavily into each of the white-populated wards in the classic machine's inner-city primary base of electoral support. Even in Mayor Daley's own Eleventh Ward there was a substantial decline in Daley's plurality. In the preceding 1959 election, Daley's plurality had been 16,355. Against Adamowski, however, his plurality fell to 10,685, a decline of 35 percent.

The other white-populated wards lacked the "hometown boy" factor to offset Adamowski's challenge, and therefore they experienced even more precipitous declines in plurality production. The powerful Thirty-first Ward, run it seems forever by the Thomas Keane family—father, then son, and now wife of son, while son completes a five-year federal jail sentence—had its 1959 plurality for Daley cut in half, falling from 14,945 to 7,503. In the Fourteenth Ward, which sits next to Daley's Eleventh, the decline was a phenomenal 67 percent, from 12,615 to 4,141.

Of course Daley did manage to win handily enough. So the question becomes, where did Daley offset the damage Adamowski caused in the machine's white-populated primary support base? He did it in the black-populated inner-city wards which made up the rest of the classic machine's primary base of support. In sharp contrast, none of these wards showed any signs of defection to Adamowski. Indeed, throughout the entire city there were only five wards which produced an increase in plurality for Daley in 1963 compared to their 1959 performance. Four of the five wards were members of the machine's classic black, inner-city base.[16] Thus, with the chips down, the black-populated wards came through with a solid display of support for Daley.

Against this backdrop, the results of the following mayoral general election in 1967 are striking in the contrast they provide. Whereas in all of Mayor Daley's previous elections the machine's main plurality-production wards were located in the inner city, in the 1967 election over one-quarter of Daley's primary base of support was located outside the inner city. Even more significant, all of the four inner-city wards which were no longer represented among the fifteen top plurality-production wards for Daley had predominantly black populations. Confirming the racial basis of the shift, the replacement wards among the top fifteen all had predominantly white populations.

Thus, the 1967 mayoral general election may be said to represent a watershed in Chicago politics. The classic inner-city base of the machine was no longer intact, and at the same time black voters no longer were among the strongest supporters of the machine's candidates for office. While the basis of politics in the city may still best be characterized as inner-city Democrats versus outer-city Republicans, race begins to displace reform as the city's cardinal political division. Table 4–2 lists the top fifteen wards for Mayor Daley in the 1967 election and an accompanying city ward map (figure 4–2) indicates the shift which occurred in the machine's primary base of electoral support.

In terms of the second distinguishing characteristic of a classic political machine, monopoly control over the primary election process, a similarly small but portentous change occurred between 1966 and 1969. As we saw earlier, the analysis by Greenstone and Peterson revealed that the machine's control over the primary election process for state representative was absolute. In 1966 and in 1968, however, two breakthroughs occurred. The first successful challenge to the machine came in an election for the office of state senator. The second victory against the machine was scored in an election for the U.S. House of Representatives. Inasmuch as these elections are more difficult to compete in than a state representative election in Illinois, the victories take on additional significance.[17]

Table 4-2
The Disintegrating Classic Machine, 1967-1969: Daley's Top Fifteen Plurality-
Producing Wards

Rank	Ward	Member of O'Connor's "Automatic Eleven"	Member of 1955-1963 Top Fifteen
1	50	no	no
2	11	no	
3	3		
4	27		
5	25	no	
6	29		
7	24		
8	31		
9	40	no	no
10	26	no	
11	49	no	no
12	20		
13	18	no	no
14	1		
15	14	no	

Source: Chicago Board of Election Commissioners.

Running on a slogan of "A Vote for Chew is a Vote for You," a black independent candidate in a district on the city's middle-class black south side broke the machine's absolute monopoly on state office. As the slogan indicates, Chew made a racial appeal to swing his black constituents away from the machine. As it turned out, however, the political significance of Chew's victory was short-lived. Upon winning, Senator Chew promptly renounced his independence for the more secure career of a machine-supporting and in turn machine-supported state senator.

That same year the machine faced another challenge, this one for election to Congress. The challenger was a machine renegade, Abner Mikva, who was giving up a machine-sponsored career as a state representative in order to contest an incumbent machine-slated congressman. In 1966 Mikva fell short of victory. However, two years later he made another bid, and this time was successful. This independent, moreover, retained his independence after winning—although the makeup of his district, which included the independently inclined areas around the University of Chicago, made this a far less precarious proposition than it was for Senator Chew.[18]

While the election of one genuine independent and the use of an appearance of independence by another candidate does not constitute much of an inroad on the machine's control over elective office, the two victories spawned a number of other independently inclined candidates to challenge what previously

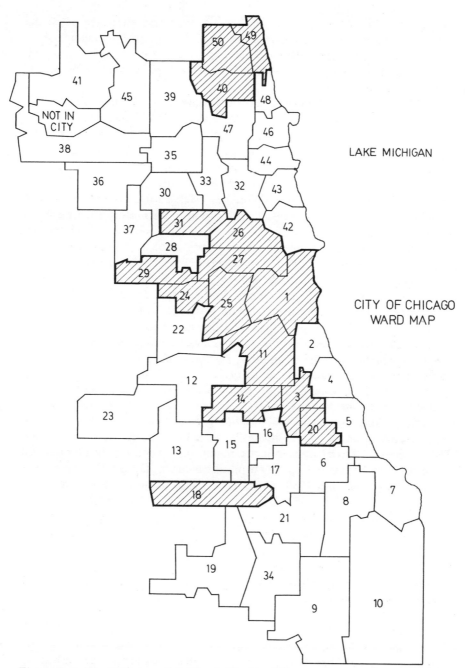

Figure 4–2. The Disintegrating Classic Machine's Primary Base of Support, 1967–1969

had appeared to be an invincible machine. A ward committeeman of the machine, Bernie Neistein, once observed "Don't back no losers." By failing to heed this advice in the sixties, the machine was to pay a heavy price during the seventies as a number of independent candidates were encouraged by the victories to take on the machine.[19]

With regard to the third characteristic we have used to distinguish a political machine in its classic form, vote size, the Daley political organization also experienced its first signs of declining strength. However, the decline here is the least significant of the three areas we are examining. While a decline can be discerned in the machine's ability to produce a large presidential vote, no such decline can be observed in the mayoral election results.

The Chicago political organization has established a national reputation, built to a large extent upon the media's attention to the massive votes the organization generates for presidential candidates. Robert Kennedy's evaluation of the organization, for example, has been widely quoted: "Daley is the whole ballgame." So it seemed in 1960, when Robert's brother John received 1,064,951 votes, and confirmation was made in 1964, when Johnson got 1,141,148 votes.

However, in the 1968 presidential election the Chicago political organization failed to deliver its standard 1 million votes. Hubert Humphrey received a considerably smaller 874,113. Of course, Humphrey had the unpopular Vietnam war hanging heavily around his shoulders, and the atrocities surrounding the 1968 Democratic National Convention that was held in Chicago undoubtedly turned some voters away from the party. Nevertheless, it is difficult to discount the entire falloff, amounting to 23 percent from the Johnson vote and 18 percent from the Kennedy vote.

On the other hand, the 1967 mayoral general election suggests that a substantial proportion of the Humphrey vote falloff can be discounted. Mayor Daley received 792,183 votes in that election, the largest vote he ever received. Since the Republicans put up only a token candidate, Daley's 1967 vote is best compared to his vote in 1959, a year when the Republicans also fielded an insignificant candidate. In 1959 Daley received 778,612. Thus, while the political organization had difficulty delivering for Humphrey, no such problem existed in regard to its main concern, reelecting Daley.

School Politics during the Transitional
Machine Period: 1966–1969

In 1966, the Daley political organization entered school politics. Thus, just as 1966 marks the beginning of the disintegration of the political organization in its classic machine form, so too does it mark the political organization's abrupt departure from a policy of noninterference in the city's schools. Moreover, the two developments are closely related, as we shall see shortly.

Despite the significance of the occasion, the media did not report the political organization's reentry into the schools. For what the organization did was to use its allies on the school board as it agents for the reintroduction of political influence. This method of influencing school-policy formation enabled the politicians, notably Mayor Daley, to reap the benefits to be derived from appearing to maintain a separation between politics and the schools, while influencing school policies in a direction that was useful to the aspirations of the political organization's leadership.

In order for the politicians to begin playing a significant role in the school policy-formation process, it was necessary to eliminate Superintendent Willis, who would not tolerate any external influence on the schools. However, by 1966 his removal no longer represented a difficult task for the politicians. The schools' racial problems had become so serious that they were spilling over the reform barriers erected around the city's schools and causing discord throughout the city. For the politicians, the problem had become intolerable. The broad and stable ethnic/racial coalition which the political organization had been able to rely upon for support since the 1930s appeared to be coming rapidly asunder. Fortunately for the politicians, the city's businessmen also had come to view the once highly regarded Willis as a liability because of his inability to restore order in the schools.[20]

Accordingly, after providing solid support for Willis's segregationist school policies throughout the early 1960s, the political organization's allies on the school board dropped their support in the fall of 1965. Thus, Willis's superintendency was brought to a close the following year.[21]

Choosing a successor was no simple matter, for a great deal was at stake. On the one hand, the new superintendent had to be a widely recognized reformer. Otherwise, charges would be leveled that the schools seemed destined to return to the terrible days of political domination. It also was important that the successor be liberal on the race issue in order to avoid the condemnation that Willis's racially discriminatory policies were to remain in effect and that therefore the city would remain in turmoil.

On the other hand, the politicians undoubtedly had had enough of autonomy in the schools, and they were anxious to play a role in the school-policy process, if only to forestall any potential disasters in the future. If Daley needed any advice on the undesirability of reform, Willis had taught him all he needed to know. Additionally, the leadership of the political organization was determined that the city's schools would remain segregated. Otherwise, there would be a continuing exodus of whites from the city, which in turn would endanger the white leadership of the political organization.[22]

In contrast to Willis's strong conservatism, what the political organization needed was a weak liberal, and, as it turned out, that is what the city's schools got. The new superintendent, James Redmond, possessed impeccable reform and liberal credentials. He had been a top aide to Herold Hunt when Hunt

superintended Chicago's schools, and subsequently had served as the superintendent of the New Orleans schools while they were undergoing court-ordered
racial integration. Thus, Redmond had experience with Chicago's schools and
with the integration problem as well.

Redmond also possessed a redeeming political virtue, which the newspapers
identified shortly after the new superintendent's arrival. The reporters characterized him as "Gentleman Jim" and "Redmond the conciliator." Redmond's views
and behavior revealed him to be no less committed to the avoidance of conflict
and the need for compromise solutions than the leadership of the political organization and the political leadership's allies on the school board.[23]

Consequently, the selection of Redmond as superintendent virtually assured
two significant outcomes. The politicians would play a major role in the schools'
policy-formation process. In contrast to Willis's dictatorial manner, Redmond's
conciliatory style committed him to deferring to the school board, and through
their allies on the school board, the politicians would therefore be able once
again to strongly influence school policies.

The city's schools would remain segregated as well. Although Redmond did
develop a comprehensive plan for the integration of the schools shortly after
his arrival, the school board elected to implement no significant policies in this
area. Redmond, in turn, anxious to avoid any appearance of conflict with the
board, elected to further investigate the problem, devise revisions, and submit
variations on the integration theme for the board's further consideration, rather
than meet the board's obvious reluctance more directly and forcefully.

The other major thrust which the political organization made into the
city's schools in 1966 was to arrange for the grant of collective-bargaining
rights to the teachers. Once again, it was the political organization's allies on the
school board who dramatically reversed themselves. After years of voicing
adamant objections to the teacher union's request for bargaining rights, the
party's allies suddenly changed their minds as soon as the mayor made it clear
that such a change was in order.

What the leadership of the political organization principally intended to
accomplish by granting bargaining rights was to gain the teachers' political
support or at least to neutralize their opposition to the political organization.
Just as it was important to remove Willis because of the racial controversy, it
was important to influence the teachers' behavior regarding the controversy.
First of all, the teachers were the only significant group of public employees in
the city who were not subject to the behavioral constraints of the political
organization's patronage system. Thus, they were free to act as they pleased
on the volatile issue. Then, too, there were a number of reformers in the leadership and membership of the union who, if given the opportunity, might force
the union into the controversy.[24] Thus, collective bargaining was expected to
transform the teachers into trade unionists who, through the process of contract
negotiations, would become beholden to the politicians for the benefits they
received.

However, the politicians once again covered their bet, so to speak, much in the same manner as they had with the recruitment of Superintendent Redmond. The politicians were relying upon the leadership of the teachers' union to defer to them, in the same way that Redmond was expected to defer to the school board. Therefore, although collective bargaining represented in principle a powerful organizational weapon, the politicians did not anticipate that the union would exploit its full potential. Indeed, as we saw in chapter 2, the perceptions of the politicians concerning the moderate and deferential character of the union leadership were altogether accurate. The conciliatory union leadership persisted in deferring to the politicians until it was driven from office.

As for the teachers' political support, as soon as collective-bargaining rights had been conferred upon the union, the leadership of the union immediately took up a strong advocacy role for the party, particularly Mayor Daley. Indeed, the union newspaper during the years 1967 to 1972, the length of the moderate leadership's term of office, reads as though its staff were on the payroll of the political organization rather than the teachers' union. Prominent news and editorial coverage of Mayor Daley, often accompanied by photos, was regularly featured in the newspaper. When the first three contract settlements between the union and the board were reached, between 1967 and 1969, the mayor's role as a mediator was abundantly and lavishly praised.

Removing all doubt about the new political commitments of the teachers' union, in 1967 the union newspaper announced the formation of a "nonpartisan committee for the reelection of Mayor Daley." The announcement was accompanied by a captioned photo of the union's leadership, stating that the leadership would be heading up the mayor's reelection bid among the teachers. During the next mayoral election, the newspaper announced that the teachers' union would channel its political support for Daley through the All-Chicago Labor Committee.[25] Thus, within a brief span of five years, the teachers' union had moved from being an independent, generally reform-oriented organization into becoming a component of the political organization's organized labor electoral apparatus.

The New Political Organization: 1970-1978

As we have seen, during the late 1960s the Daley political organization began to lose some of its classic machine characteristics and some of its organizational strength. In view of the nature of the losses, it seems evident that the civil-rights crisis in the schools, along with other racially discriminatory policies that we have not discussed, were principal factors in the alteration of the political organization.[26] During the 1970s the alteration and declining strength of the Daley political organization continued unabated. Finally, by the mid-1970s the organization no longer possessed any of the chief characteristics or the strength of a classic political machine. According to each of the tests we have applied to distinguish a classic machine, the Chicago political organization during the 1970s has become a substantially altered and far less powerful form of political organization.

This is not to say that the Chicago political party is no longer formidable; it is still by far the strongest political organization in the city. What is being argued is that big-city political organizations everywhere have declined in strength, and the Chicago party is no exception. The Chicago political organization no longer possesses a solid bloc of inner-city wards, as it did until the late 1960s, upon which it can rely to deliver massive pluralities for any and all candidates slated for office by the party. Additionally, the organization is no longer capable of maintaining even a slight resemblance of monopoly control over Democratic primary elections. Finally, as for the tremendous vote which the party in its classic form had been able to invariably deliver, the new political organization seems incapable of generating a similarly large vote even under favorable circumstances.

Consider the Chicago political organization's monopoly in the inner-city wards. At the outset of Daley's mayoral term, the political organization's main plurality-production wards were all located in the inner city. Now, however, nine of the inner-city wards which had made up the classic base of the machine are no longer represented among the top-fifteen production wards. Moreover, whereas at the outset all of the city's black wards were among the top-fifteen producers for Daley, now only one black ward remains among the top producers.[27]

The characteristics of the Chicago political organization's new primary base of electoral support reflect the extent to which race has come to play a central role in the city's politics. Over half of the party's new base of support is located on the southwest side of the city. This area is populated by blue-collar whites, who of course are in the most direct competition with the city's black residents for employment, housing, schooling, and numerous other benefits. The bulk of the city's black population is located east of this area, and over the years blacks gradually, and with great difficulty, have been moving westward. The movement has driven a number of whites to the suburbs, which in turn erodes the political organization's new primary base of electoral support.[28]

Table 4–3 and the accompanying city ward map (figure 4–3) indicate the radical transformation which the Chicago political organization has undergone during the 1970s. In contrast to the party basis of the city's politics which existed earlier, inner-city Democrats versus outer-city Republicans, it now seems more accurate to characterize the basis as racial.

The Chicago political organization's other characteristic of classic machine control, monopolization of the Democratic primary election process, also has undergone considerable change. Greenstone and Peterson reported that between 1958 and 1964, the party's monopoly was complete. During the late 1960s we saw some minor evidence of a break in the monopoly. By 1978, however, the party has been challenged in almost every district in the city. Now, in nine of

Table 4-3
The New Political Organization, 1970-1978: Daley's Top Fifteen Plurality-Producing Wards

Rank	Ward	Member of O'Connor's "Automatic Eleven"	Member of 1955-1963 Top Fifteen
1	11		yes
2	31	yes	yes
3	12		
4	13		
5	14		yes
6	36		
7	18		
8	26		yes
9	19		
10	23		
11	25		yes
12	10		
13	27	yes	yes
14	15		
15	38		

Source: Chicago Board of Election Commissioners.

the city's twenty legislative districts, independents have gained state representative office. Moreover, in three of the nine districts, independents have won the more difficult to achieve office of state senator as well as the representative seat.

Adding insult to this serious injury, independents have challenged the political organization in an additional seven districts during the 1970s. Of the seven challenges, over half have been creditable efforts. The best of the losing efforts was a loss by 300 votes in 1976, made by a candidate who had the support of an independent steelworkers' union. In 1978 the candidate ran again and won. Thus, in a span of eight years, the political party has been successfully or closely challenged in well over half of the city's legislative districts.

The legislative elections also lend confirmation to what we observed earlier about the new primary base of electoral support for the political organization. Of the four remaining districts in the city where the party has been able to maintain monopoly control, three are located on the southwest side. This, of course, corresponds to the party's shift in primary electoral support for Daley. Thus, in both instances the new political organization finds its most loyal supporters in the most racially troubled white sections of the city.[29]

In the third area where we earlier observed evidence of the existence of a classic political machine in Chicago, vote size, once again the 1970s data show a remarkable variation from the earlier pattern, which is consistent with the other 1970s electoral data we have examined. During the 1950s and early 1960s, the

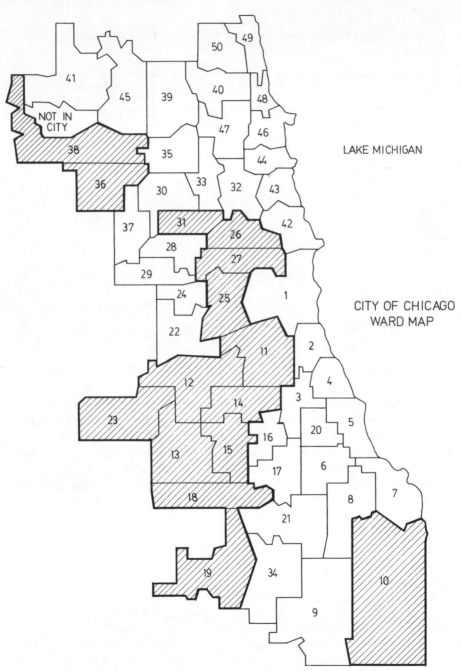

Figure 4-3. The New Political Organization's Primary Base of Support, 1970-1978

political organization was able to produce a consistently large vote in national as well as local elections. Then, in the late 1960s we discerned some decline in the presidential vote for Humphrey. However, Mayor Daley's vote during the same time period remained as large as ever. In contrast, by the mid-1970s the political organization was not producing its traditional massive vote in either local or national elections.

In order to demonstrate the severity of the decline in the party's electoral strength, we shall present both mayoral and presidential election results for the years 1955 to 1977. The mayoral election data (see table 4-4) reveal three different aspects of the political organization's declining electoral strength. First, there has been a steady decline since 1967. Yet, in all three of Daley's last elections and that of his successor, Michael Bilandic, the Republicans were only able to field minor candidates. The Republican organization itself barely exists within the city's limits, being much more a suburban operation. Therefore, it seems reasonable to conclude that the basis for the party's declining vote rests more within the political organization than with the quality of the opposition.

The second and third aspects of the party's declining strength can be seen in both the 1975 and 1977 results. First, there is a decline of nearly 200,000 votes for Daley in 1975 from his previous election, and an even larger decline in 1977 for Bilandic. No less remarkable, over half of the city's fifty wards failed to deliver their standard 10,000+ vote for Daley in 1975, and nearly two-thirds failed to do so for Bilandic in 1977. Even when Daley was strongly opposed in 1955 and 1963, he maanged to get at least 10,000 votes from nearly all of the city's wards. Thus, the decline in the organization's strength in the mid-1970s is widespread as well as substantial.

Table 4-4
Chicago Mayoral General Election Totals, 1955–1977

Year	Democrat	Republican Opponent	Number of Wards with fewer than 10,000 Democratic Votes
1955	708,222	581,555	2
1959	778,612	311,940	none
1963	679,497	540,705	5
1967	792,283	272,542	none
1971	740,137	315,969	3
1975	542,817	139,335	26
1977	490,688	135,282	32

Source: Chicago Board of Election Commissioners.

The presidential election returns (see table 4-5) offer confirmation of the organization's declining strength during the 1970s. We already have considered some of the reasons why the turnout for Humphrey may have been lower than usual, namely the Vietnam war and the violence at the 1968 Democratic National Convention. It may be possible to account for McGovern's poor showing on the basis of the Daley delegates being ousted from the Democratic National Convention in Miami. Speculation was raised in the media that the McGovern people supported the ouster, and some of the political organization's committeemen indicated they would not be supporting McGovern.

However, when it comes to the Carter vote, no obvious excuses are available. Carter had no albatrosses hanging around his neck which may have deterred the organization or the voters from supporting his candidacy. Indeed, the city's black vote for Carter was extraordinarily high.[30] Yet, despite the unusual swell of black voters, the organization was unable to deliver many more votes for Carter than it did for McGovern, and the Carter vote was nearly 100,000 below Humphrey's. Thus, it would appear that even under favorable circumstances, the Daley political organization no longer is capable of delivering the kind of vote for which it used to receive national attention.

School Politics during the New Political Organization Period: 1970-1978

When Mayor Daley first was elected to office in 1955, his principal concern with regard to the city's schools was to maintain a clear separation between them and the activities of the political organization. At that time Daley needed to establish a reputation as a reformer in order to gain the confidence of the city's business and reform interests. In any event, the schools did not provide any signficant inducements to encourage political intervention.

Table 4-5
Chicago Presidential General Election Totals, 1956-1976

Year	Democrat	Republican	Candidates
1956	807,174	849,241	Stevenson vs. Eisenhower
1960	1,064,951	608,639	Kennedy vs. Nixon
1964	1,141,148	466,296	Johnson vs. Goldwater
1968	874,113	452,914	Humphrey vs. Nixon
1972	758,489	556,373	McGovern vs. Nixon
1976	776,539	375,165	Carter vs. Ford

Source: Chicago Board of Election Commissioners.

However, by the mid-1960s the schools' political attributes had changed considerably. A civil-rights controversy emerged and then got decidedly out of hand; at the same time, the teachers suddenly became more militant, even threatening to strike unless they were granted collective-bargaining rights. From the politicians' point of view, these problems represented strong inducements to reestablish political influence over the schools. Accordingly, Daley approved the school board's hiring of a more politicaly amenable superintendent in order to terminate the civil-rights problem, and the granting of collective-bargaining rights to the teachers in order to gain the teachers' political support.

Both solutions worked very effectively. Order was restored in the city's schools, and the politicians gained a significant measure of influence over both the school policy-formation process and the teachers' union. The new superintendent, while presenting a plan to integrate the city's schools, deferred to the school board's judgment to do little about implementing his proposals. As for collective bargaining, Daley easily mediated the first two contract settlements, and, after some difficulty, he mediated the third settlement, thereby gaining recognition from the teachers as the principal source of their benefits.

However, in the 1970s both of the politicians' solutions began to come awry. It turned out that not only was Superintendent Redmond incapable of implementing an integration plan (a perfectly acceptable failing as far as the politicians were concerned), but Redmond was unable to deal effectively with a good many other problems as well. Most notably, the superintendent was an ineffectual negotiator with the teachers' union, and by the 1970s this weakness was no longer acceptable to the politicians. The funds required to finance generous settlements were becoming far more difficult for the politicians to obtain. Thus, Redmond's ineffectual style of leadership turned into a liability instead of an asset as the nature of the schools' central problem changed.[31]

The basic problem with the teachers' union was that elements within the union's leadership had become increasingly less willing to defer to the politicians in determining an acceptable level of contract benefits. When the leadership of the union changed hands in 1972, the politicians suddenly were confronted by a union that intended to dictate the terms of contract settlement. Indeed, from 1973 onward, the union imposed settlements without regard to either the preferences of the politicians or the ability of the school board to finance the settlements.

Thus, the solutions reached by the politicians in 1966 wound up producing major problems of their own by the 1970s. The politicians dealt with the superintendency problem in the same manner as they had earlier. A new superintendent was hired, and this one, Joseph Hannon, was well suited to his principal task—the union—in the same way that Redmond had been well suited to removing integration from the city's school agenda.

It became evident early that Hannon was likely to be an altogether different type of superintendent. To begin, the school board broke its tradition of hiring an "outsider." Hannon was recruited from within the management ranks of the city's schools, whereas Hunt, Willis, and Redmond had all been well-recognized superintendents of other big-city school systems. Hannon also was not a reformer in the conventional sense, nor was he a graduate of one of the leading schools of education. Consequently, Hannon does not possess the high standing of his predecessors among professional educators.[32]

What all of this means is that Hannon very likely will perform as an agent of the politicians. Through their influence on the school board, the politicians created Hannon's career as a superintendent. Therefore it is with the politicians, rather than the reform "tradition," that Hannon's loyalties lie. In turn, then, it is not Hannon's task to reform the schools, since the politicians have little interest in such an objective. Rather, it is his task to reduce the influence of the teachers' union over the schools, and to thereby return a measure of control to the politicians via their representatives on the school board.[33]

To be sure, Hannon's task is not simple, nor can the superintendent rely on consistent support from the politicians. During Hannon's first negotiating session with the teachers' union in 1975, Hannon and the school board elected to hold firm in the face of a two-week strike by the union. However, the strike ended when Mayor Daley suddenly intervened (without the school board asking him to) to impose a settlement which, as we saw earlier, included all of the union's demands. What the politicians are unwilling to do in attempting to break the union's hold on the schools is to have it appear that they are attempting to do so. Therefore, the politicians can only support Hannon's actions up to a point. The unions and the politicians, after all, have a close relationship in Chicago, as is true in a majority of big cities. Accordingly, dealing with the powerful public employee unions is a complex and delicate task, since the politicians seek to avoid any appearance of engaging in union "busting."[34]

As for the politicians' other problem, dealing directly with the union's increasing strength and independence, no effective solutions so far have been presented. As we saw in chapter 2, in 1973 and 1975 Mayor Daley allowed the teachers to remain out on strike for two weeks in an effort to test the ability of the union to maintain an effective strike and to turn public opinion against the union. Yet in both instances the mayor ultimately felt compelled to intervene and produce a settlement in accordance with the union's terms.

To make matters worse, the political support that the political organization had been receiving from the union no longer is forthcoming at the local level since the leadership of the union changed hands in 1972. This change is particularly interesting because it indicates the close relationship which has developed between the two phenomena we are examining: the decline of the big-city political organization and the emergence of powerful public employee unions, resulting in union rule.

On the one hand, regardless of whether the teacher union leadership is inclined to provide the local party with union support, as the moderate union leadership did in 1967 and 1971 when the union endorsed Mayor Daley, such support is more difficult to provide in the 1970s. This is because both of the two groups with whom the party has increasingly lost favor in the city, blacks and liberals, are well represented in the teachers' union. In general, given their income and education level, teachers possess the same characteristics as those voters who increasingly have tended to support independent candidates for office in Chicago. Moreover, blacks make up 40 percent of the teaching staff, and they have formed an effective caucus within the union to promote and protect black interests.[35]

Thus, in 1975 when Daley was confronted by an extraordinary challenge in the mayoral primary, the union newspaper virtually ignored the election and made no endorsement of the mayor. The same thing occurred in the 1977 special mayoral election following Daley's death. In both instances, the political organization was being challenged by prominent black candidates, while in the 1975 primary a white liberal ran and in the 1977 special election a white with substantial ethnic backing was in the race. Thus, the leadership would have been hard pressed to secure an endorsement for Daley, and the effort certainly would have created discord within the union.[36]

On the other hand, the union leadership no longer is as inclined as it once was to provide the local party with political support. The union to a great extent has outgrown local politics, so to speak. In 1966 when the union acquired collective-bargaining rights, its membership numbered just over 13,000. John Desmond, the union president elected in 1966 to replace John Fewkes, was nearly sixty years of age and had served with Fewkes as a union official for a number of years. In addition to his advanced age and long service in the local union, in the words of Paul Peterson, Desmond "was almost a carbon copy of the mayor himself. Irish, Catholic, short, fat, good-humored, pragmatic, realistic, he understood the language of working people and machine politicians."[37] To use Robert Merton's distinction, the president of the small teachers' union possessed a local rather than a cosmopolitan orientation.

However, by 1975 the union's membership had more than doubled, to in excess of 29,000.[38] Moreover, the current head of the union, Robert Healy, is a far more powerful figure than Desmond ever was. Healy is the president of the state teachers' union, the Illinois Federation of Teachers; a highly influential vice-president of the national teachers' union, the American Federation of Teachers; and he regularly serves as an elected delegate to the AFL-CIO. Accordingly, whereas the union's newspaper once extolled the virtues of Mayor Daley on a regular basis, now the paper rarely mentions the party's mayor. Instead the newspaper now carries frequent accounts of the activities and aspirations of Albert Shanker, the president of the AFT, and much more mention than before of state, national, and AFL-CIO politics and issues.[39]

A central reason for the broader orientation of the union's current leadership involves money. The funds that have financed the teachers' contracts never have been appropriated at the lcoal level, but at the state level, and, if the teachers' unions have their way, in the future a significant proportion of funding will come from the federal level. Thus, as the union leadership has gained sophistication, its interests have come to focus on the sources of the union's well-being. Indeed, while the union's political activities at the local level have greatly diminished, at the state and federal levels its political activities have significantly increased. In 1975 the union announced the formation of a separate political activity organization. The organization is funded by voluntary contributions from the union's membership at a rate of $2 per member a year. According to the union newspaper, in 1976 the fund contained $56,000, making the teachers' union one of the most powerful political financiers in the state.[40]

What the union has done with the money also shows the extent to which its ties with the local political party have diminished. The union in 1975 did endorse the entire statewide slate of the Democratic organization, and the slate mainly was the doing of the Chicago political organization. However, the legislative candidates endorsed by the union included Republicans as well as Democrats, liberals as well as reactionaries, and independents as well as regular party candidates. As the union newspaper emphasized, the endorsements were based solely on a candidate's voting record on education bills.[41]

Thus, whereas the early union leadership relied upon the local political organization to secure the funds needed to finance teachers' benefits, the current leadership of the union has taken the matter of securing funding directly into the union's hands, and in a highly effective manner. Illinois legislators agree that the education lobby is by far one of the most powerful actors in state politics. In a short span of ten years, then, the teachers' union has moved from a position of dependence on the Chicago political organization to the point where it now takes for granted the support of the organization while forging broader alliances of its own at the same time.

Notes

1. Edward Banfield and James Q. Wilson, *City Politics* (New York: Vintage Books, 1963), p. 214.

2. Sterling Spero and John M. Capozzola, *The Urban Community and Its Unionized Bureaucrats: Pressure Politics in Local Government Labor Relations* (New York: Dunellen, 1973), pp. 13–39.

3. Theodore Lowi, "Gosnell's Chicago Revisited via Lindsay's New York," foreword to the second edition, in Harold Gosnell, *Machine Politics: Chicago Model* (Chicago: University of Chicago Press, 1968).

4. Ibid., p. xiv.

5. The three phases are incipient, moderate, and fully developed union rule. During the incipient stage, an increasing number of union delegates gradually

came to support the effort to secure collective bargaining. Finally, by 1966 the radical delegates possessed just enough strength to force a showdown with the union's conservative leadership.

6. J. David Greenstone and Paul E. Peterson, "Reformers, Machines, and the War on Poverty," in James Q. Wilson, ed., *City Politics and Public Policy* (New York: John Wiley and Sons, 1968). Also, see the chapter on the machine in Banfield and Wilson, *City Politics.*

7. The figure is based on a conventional rule-of-thumb calculation that multiplies the estimated number of patronage workers by ten to arrive at a patronage vote. The ten takes into account family, friends, and neighbors of the patronage worker. An effective ward committeeman makes it a point to check on whether a patronage worker's family voted, and virtually all precinct captains have vote quotas they are expected to fulfill.

8. Len O'Connor, *Clout: Mayor Daley and His City* (New York: Avon Books, 1975).

9. Ibid., p. 177.

10. Greenstone and Peterson, "Reformers and Machines."

11. All of the electoral data reported here is from the Chicago Board of Election Commissioners, unless otherwise specified.

12. In 1955, 1957, 1959, and 1966 the political organization supported school construction bond issues, and the construction was conducted without scandal. Thus, the party could be perceived as genuinely concerned about the schools and honest to boot. See Mary J. Herrick, *The Chicago Schools: A Social and Political History* (Beverly Hills, Cal.: Sage Publications, 1971), p. 309.

13. Marion Byrnes and Nicholas Cannella, *136 Years of Teaching in Chicago* (Chicago: Chicago Teachers' Union, no date). A vivid portrayal of the radical and reformist Chicago Teachers' Union during the 1930s is provided by Robert J. Braun, *Teachers and Power: The Story of the American Federation of Teachers* (New York: Simon and Schuster, 1972), pp. 42–48.

14. Herrick, *Chicago Schools,* describes the close relationship between the union leadership and Superintendents Hunt and Willis.

15. Len O'Connor, *Clout,* carries an interesting account of Adamowski as well as the Daley–Adamowski election.

16. The four black wards were the Second, Third, Fourth, and Sixth. Interestingly, the lone white ward was the liberal Fifth located around the University of Chicago; the Fifth Ward does, however, have a sizable black population.

17. In Illinois, three state representatives are elected from each legislative district, and voters are entitled to cast up to three votes for a single candidate. In all other elections, candidates may receive only a single vote, and thus they must possess broader backing.

18. Not long after Abner Mikva won the congressional seat, the area was redistricted, forcing Mikva to move to Evanston.

19. The leadership of the independent political movement in Chicago is small and the leaders communicate regularly with each other. Thus, a victory or good effort in one district or ward has an immediate "multiplier effect."

20. Willis's loss of support from the business community is described in Stephen D. London, *Business and the Chicago Public School System, 1890–1966*, (Ph.D. dissertation, University of Chicago, 1968).

21. The school board renewed Willis's contract for four years in 1965. However, an understanding was reached that he would retire the following year at age 65, even though there were no age limitations on the superintendency. Thus, the school board moved on Willis as quietly as possible in light of the controversy and Willis's strong support from white parents opposed to integration.

22. At the time, and even today, the top hierarchy of the political organization is almost entirely white, and mainly Irish.

23. Paul Peterson has described Redmond as a traditional educator who had a deeply ingrained need "to perceive himself as the leader of a united educational community, who had to protect the interests of his professional associates vis-à-vis outsiders." See Peterson, *School Politics*, pp. 201–202.

24. Additionally, in 1966 approximately 30 percent of Chicago's school teachers were black.

25. *Chicago Union Teacher*, March 1967, February 1971.

26. In addition to the schools' racial problems, the city administration had major lawsuits charging racial discrimination in the police department, fire department, and in public housing. After lengthly litigation, the city lost all of the suits.

27. The sole black ward remaining among the top-fifteen producers is the Twenty-seventh. Its committeeman is white, though.

28. In 1976 Mayor Daley issued an order that all city employees must reside within the city limits. Most of those affected by the order were whites who had moved to the suburbs. Their forced return has had the effect of stabilizing the southwest and northwest sides of the city, and thereby aiding the white leadership of the party. On the other hand, a number of prominent white party leaders are moving to the suburbs to establish more racially secure bases. The most prominent mover is Morgan Finley, a former neighbor of Daley's who moved from the Eleventh Ward to a western suburb and is in the process of seeking a committeeman's position. Finley heads the patronage-rich Circuit Court of Chicago.

29. One district is on the far north side, the Fifteenth; the districts on the southwest side are the Twenty-third, Twenty-fifth, and Twenty-eight.

30. Six wards in the city produced over 20,000 votes for Carter. Of the six, four were black wards. Daley's patronage-laden Eleventh Ward was one of the two white wards.

31. Redmond's ineffectual negotiating with the teachers' union is discussed in detail in Chapter 5.

32. Hannon was the school system's director of facilities planning before becoming superintendent.

33. Hannon has been highly critical on several occasions of policies that afford the teachers too much protection and provide for too little accountability. In response to a reporter's question as to whether any Chicago principals or teachers had been fired for not performing effectively, Hannon replied, "Oh, yes we have. I don't want to come on as a hatchet man. If I come out with a statistic like that, they'll say he's more concerned with firing teachers than he is with quality education. We are starting to put more accountability into our schools, but due process—it's killing us. It's a constraint. . . . to get rid of a teacher will cost us as much as $30,000 to $35,000." *Chicago Daily News,* April 6, 1977. For a comparison with Redmond's style of conciliation, see Paul Peterson's characterization of Redmond in note 23.

34. Criticizing unions has long been the preserve of the far political right. Even the liberal reformers in Chicago are reluctant to make such criticism, and a number of the liberals are closely associated with unions. Dealing with the public unions therefore requires a wrenching ideological shift for not only the political party but the party's liberal opposition as well.

35. "Administrative and Teaching Personnel Racial Survey" (Chicago: Board of Education, January 8, 1975).

36. I have been informed by several people within the union that an effort by some of the union's leadership to secure an endorsement of the party's candidate in the special mayoral election in 1977 was thwarted by the black caucus.

37. Peterson, *School Politics,* p. 192.

38. Byrne and Cannella, *136 Years of Teaching.*

39. When Shanker ousted David Selden from the American Federation of Teachers' presidency in 1974, Healy played a highly supportive role. Healy was able to deliver virtually all 220 Illinois delegates for Shanker. *Chicago Tribune,* August 20, 1974.

40. *Chicago Union Teacher,* December 1976.

41. Ibid, October 1976.

5

The Politicians' Relationship to the Schools under Union Rule

Introduction

The substantial and broad range of benefits acquired by the teachers under union rule was described in chapter 3. Chapter 4 went on to examine the circumstances under which union rule developed in the schools. It was shown that the emergence and subsequent development of union rule corresponds to a decline in the organizational strength and form of the political party.

In view of the extent to which these two developments parallel one another, it is now necessary to examine more closely the actual relationship which exists between the politicians and the school policy-formation process. Accordingly, in this chapter we shall analyze the means by which and the extent to which the politicians have been able to influence school policy in the area of collective bargaining. In Harold Lasswell's terms, we shall determine "how" the politicians have managed to alter school policy so that the teachers have become the primary beneficiaries of the city's public schools.

In order to make the determination, the level of political activity and penetration will be examined for each of the four primary channels of access into the school policy-formation process. These channels are the school board member-selection committee, school board officers, school management, and individual school board members. Should the politicians attempt to influence school policy, the influence very likely would be conveyed through one or more of the four primary channels of entry.

It should be pointed out before beginning the inquiry that there is virtually universal agreement among educators and political scientists that the schools are autonomous to an exceptionally high degree. Therefore, the influence channels just described should admit little or no external access to the policy-formation process. What the studies of school politics almost invariably have found, particularly in regard to the much more complex big-city school systems, is that school administrators dominate the policy-formation process. Thus, in a review of the politics-of-education literature, Paul Peterson concluded that the twin tenets of the conventional wisdom concerning the schools are their autonomy and their dominance by school management.[1]

Yet, as we shall see here, this is no longer the case with Chicago's schools. However, the exceptional situation of Chicago's schools should not simply be dismissed as further evidence that Chicago's politics are unique. Actually, under reform rule, between 1947 and 1965, Chicago's schools did conform to the

conventional pattern of autonomy and managerial dominance, despite the fact
that a powerful political party existed during this period. Indeed, one Chicago
school superintendent of this period, Benjamin Willis, has been characterized
as having "exhibited the type of personal, political, and professional dominance
seldom found on the American educational scene."[2]

Chicago's schools broke with the conventional pattern, however, following
the grant of collective bargaining to the teachers in 1966. Union rule proceeded
to develop in the schools. Therefore, it is not a matter of Chicago's unique
political party making the Chicago schools exceptional. Rather, it is the emergence of union rule which accounts for the radical transformation. Accordingly,
it may well be that in other big-city school politics, and bureau politics in
general, there has been a similar transformation as a result of the development
of union rule. In any event, to the extent that union rule develops within a
bureaucracy, autonomy and managerial dominance no longer will characterize
the bureaucracy's politics or policy making.

School board member selection constitutes an initial and vital channel
of influence into the schools. As Robert Crain and James Vanecko concluded
in their eight-city study of school desegregation policy formation, if the back-
grounds of the school board members can be determined, then policy outcomes
can be predicted with a considerable degree of accuracy.[3] It is interesting
to note that the most prominent studies of city politics during the 1960s did
not place much emphasis on this indirect form of influence. The two most
notable studies, by Robert Dahl and Edward Banfield, both focused almost
exclusively upon influence which was conveyed at the time a decision was being
made.[4]

Yet, from what Crain and Vanecko as well as others have found, it is clear
that if sufficient care is taken in the selection of decision makers, then matters
largely take care of themselves later on.[5] Indeed, when politicians involve
themselves at the time a decision is being made, this may actually indicate that
the bureau or other location where the decision is being made is underpoliticized
rather than overpoliticized. If the selection process had been well-politicized,
so to speak, then there would be little need for the politicians to involve themselves in subsequent decisions.

Another critical pipeline of influence into the school policy-formation
process is the school board's officers. A school board's chief officer, in particular,
typically comes to possess a considerable degree of influence over fellow board
members. Unlike the other board members, the chief officer is kept informed
of day-to-day developments, he has the authority to make decisions between
meetings of the board, and as a result, he comes to possess much greater knowledge about and influence over the affairs of the board. Other board members
frequently defer, then, not only to the chief officer's formal authority, but to
his informal authority as well. Accordingly, whoever has the chief officer's ear
typically can influence far more than the chief officers's behavior.

The chief officer also appoints committee chairmen and other committee members, which lends additional political importance to the chief officer's role. By appointing chairmen who are in sympathy with his views, a chief officer can consolidate his authority. A chief officer's appointments also enhance or diminish the prospect of benefits for those who are affected by a subcommittee's determination. Then, too, appointments can be made with or without regard to the interests of the politicians. Under union rule, the most important committee of the school board is of course the collective-bargaining committee. Therefore, we shall devote particular attention to the membership and behavior of this committee.

A third critical political conduit is the school superintendent. As the big-city schools became more reformed and complex, the influence of the superintendent has increased substantially. The currency of school politics under reform rule, after all, is knowledge, and as the school system's chief expert, the superintendent came to possess a good deal of capital.

When the reformers separated the schools from the city's politics, two formidable taboos were promulgated, and these taboos often were used by the superintendents to elevate their influence over that of the school board's. The first taboo involves the distinction between lay and professional knowledge and judgment. The distinction provides a superintendent with the opportunity to characterize board-member inquiries and directives as being either misinformed lay or dangerous political encroachments upon his professional domain. The second taboo involves a similar distinction between policy formulation and policy implementation. The former is the board's proper concern, while the latter falls within the responsibility of management. Both distinctions are of course highly judgmental, and since the managers are the experts, their judgments often carry the greatest weight. Yet, turning over too much responsibility to management may leave the board in a position of making policy announcements rather than policy decisions.[6]

The final channel of access into the schools is through individual board members. By voting, boards determine which policies ultimately will be implemented. The policy which union-rule politicians perceive to be of paramount importance is collective bargaining, and contract settlements come up annually for the full board's consideration. Since a majority vote is needed to approve a settlement, the politicians obviously are interested in having access to at least a majority of the school board's members.

Of course, as we have just said, political influence does not need to be direct nor must it occur at the time a decision is being made in order to be present and effective. A nominee to the school board may be subjected to careful evaluation and political influence at the time of selection, which serves to influence his future behavior. Other board members, notably the chief officer and pertinent committee chairmen, may serve as instruments of political influence as well. Even a school superintendent may function in such a capacity.

If need be, however, the politicians do possess resources which they can use to exert influence on board members. The reappointment factor, for example, hangs heavily over the heads of board members interested in serving an additional term, and it therefore can be manipulated to political advantage. In addition to such threats, the politicians often possess various positive means of extracting an appropriate response from board members. Board members frequently are businessmen, and businessmen typically understand that occasionally it is necessary to "go along in order to get along." Thus, in exchange for political support, a businessman may become the recipient of any number of forms of so-called "honest graft" or some other kind of political consideration. Finally, the mayor, as the city's chief officer, may encourage board members to adopt a broader or different, say a political, perspective on a given issue. Board members who could not be influenced by positive or negative sanctions may be susceptible to this type of influence.[7]

Since the onset of union rule, Chicago's politicians, principally the mayor, have used all four of the channels of influence to exert political pressure on the school policy-formation process in regard to the crucial policy of collective-bargaining contract settlements. In order to appreciate better the extent of activity and penetration by the politicians into the schools, the four channels of influence now will be considered in greater detail. As in the preceding chapters, union rule will be examined within the context of the preceding forms of urban government, machine rule and reform rule.

School Board Member Selection

As a result of the great school-accreditation scandal that rocked Chicago during the late 1940s, the city's reformers were presented with the extraordinary opportunity of establishing a landmark school reform. The reform represented a landmark in that it entailed taking away the mayor's free hand in making appointments to the school board. The novel curtailment of political influence was accomplished through the creation of an independent screening commission, composed of representatives from the city's leading businesses, civic organizations, universities, and organized labor. The commission's charge was to recruit, evaluate, and then recommend to the mayor outstanding candidates for the school board.

During earlier and less troubled times, the politicians had scoffed whenever the reformers had broached the subject of a school board screening mechanism. However, the accreditation scandal served to produce a passing marriage of convenience between the politicians and the reformers. The politicians were desperately seeking to dissociate themselves from the school scandal, in which they were deeply involved because of their highly visible influence on the schools. The reformers, on the other hand, were no less interested in involving themselves in the troubled schools. Thus, the school board screening commission served the interests of both parties. It placed the reformers, in effect, between the politicians and the schools, and from this influential vantage point the reformers would serve as the highly visible guardians of the public's interest in the schools.

The viewpoint to which the reformers were subscribing with the screening mechanism is straightforward enough: name the players, name the outcomes. While the strategy does not determine specific decisions, it does apply to the general ideological framework involved in school board policy making.[8] Thus, by submitting a list of reform-oriented nominees for the school board, the commission had the mayor hemmed in very neatly. The mayor could sort, ponder, and choose, but he invariably wound up with a reformer on his hands.

So it appeared at the outset anyway. Actually, there were three critical flaws in the reformers' grand design for gaining control over the schools. First, the advisory screening committee remained simply that: advisory. While the mayor may have solemnly pledged himself and declared it a moral necessity to abide by the advice of the commission, he never allowed himself to become legally bound by the commission's recommendations. At one point Mayor Daley did announce, after revising the commission, that he would move to grant the commission legal status if the reconstituted commission proved to be successful. However, the mayor apparently never got around to completing his evaluation, since to this day the commission remains merely advisory.[9]

The second flaw was that the reformers on the commission soon learned that a pure reform strategy was not a realistic option. The purpose of the commission was, after all, to remove political influence from the schools, not to transfer wholesale control of the schools to the reformers. Moreover, the reformers simply do not enjoy favor or possess well-credentialed allies in many areas of the city. Reform is principally a Protestant and Jewish phenomenon favored among the middle classes, while Chicago is largely a Catholic working-class city. Finally, the mayor is not likely to tolerate an undiluted flow of reform-oriented nominees from the commission. Even reform-oriented Mayor Kennelly balked, presumably at the political organization's insistence, when the commission failed to recommend a wealthy, politically well-connected Polish candidate for reappointment to the board.[10]

A third flaw perhaps has given the reformers the most concern of all. There is simply no guarantee that an individual who has all the earmarks of a reformer will wind up voting as a reformer once he is appointed to the board. In part, this is only evidence of the obvious fact that individuals are not unidimensional characters forged solely along machine or reform lines. The issues which come up for vote by the school board are at times not readily distinguishable along such lines either.

However, the greater part of the reformers' problem involves the presence of other values and pressures which impinge upon a reformer's commitments.

That old standby, material considerations, frequently comes into conflict with convictions. Racial considerations also can serve to divide white from minority reformers. Past obligations, too, may rear their head, and politicians are masters (it being a vital part of the craft) at calling in, on opportune occasions, what the Chicago politicians refer to as "due notes." Finally, there is the matter of re-appointment. At some point a reformer has to decide if it is to be "go-for-broke" reforming in which case the prospects for serving an additional term are bleak, or incremental reform, the more rational choice for a board member desirous of reappointment. The problem with the latter strategy is that the politicians well may expect some say in determining what the increments are to be.

The flaws were not readily apparent at the outset, however. Indeed, the advisory screening commission got off to a remarkably effective beginning as far as the reformers were concerned. When the commission was being established, a part of the deal with the desperate Mayor Kelly had been that all of the sitting school board members would submit their resignations. In that way the screening commission could begin with a fresh slate. However, only seven of the eleven-member Kelly board agreed to go along with the arrangement. This meant that in order to develop a reform-oriented majority on the board, the commission had to come up with and the mayor had to approve virtually a pure set of reform-oriented candidates. Astonishingly enough, that is just what happened. According to Mary Herrick, during the late 1940s and early 1950s, the vote typically came down 6–5 in favor of reform. Thus, for the first time, the Chicago school board was dominated by reformers.[11]

As it turned out, this was to be the high-water mark of the reform-oriented screening commission's influence on the school board. Following its auspicious start, the commission began to evenly divide its recommendations to the mayor along reform- and machine-oriented lines. Paul Peterson's analysis of school-board voting behavior for the years 1946–1968 indicates that the advisory screening commission produced ten machine-oriented and eleven reform-oriented voters.[12]

The shift in the orientation of the screening commission constitutes an important development. What was originally intended to be a mechanism for curtailing political influence on the schools instead became a means of accommodating and legitimizing political influence. Thus, in 1966 when the school board dramatically dropped its long-standing opposition and granted the teachers collective-bargaining rights, it was clear that the mayor was able to have his way with a majority of the school board's members. At the same time, however, the mayor bore no formal responsibility for the school board's decision. As for even influencing the school board, the mayor could plausibly deny that he possessed much influence by pointing to the reformers' screening commission which was responsible for making recommendations to him. By the mid-1960s, then, the advisory screening commission had come to serve the politicians' interests better than it served the reformers'.

In 1968, however, the advisory screening commission made it very evident that it would accommodate the politicians only up to a point. The commission failed to recommend for reappointment both the president and vice-president of the board, both of whom were among the mayor's closest and obviously strongest allies on the board. In a close and heated vote, the reformers dramatically broke the prevailing accommodation pattern.[13] The two board members whom the screening commission rejected had been strong supporters of Superintendent Willis's "neighborhood schools" policy, which had served to maintain Chicago's highly segregated school system. Both men also had played an instrumental role in thwarting Superintendent Redmond's subsequent efforts to integrate the city's schools. Additionally, both men were over seventy years of age, and both had strong ties to the city's political subservient and conservative organized-labor establishment.

Fortunately for the mayor, there were three additional appointments to be made to the school board that year. Therefore, the mayor was able to ignore the commission's rejection of his allies and reappoint both men because he could use the other three appointments to placate the blacks and reformers who were so vocal in their opposition to the president and vice-president. The admirable show of political finesse did get the mayor past the immediate disaster; however, because of the considerable media attention directed to the mayor's maneuvering, the legitimacy of the reformers' screening-commission mechanism was left in a shambles. Accordingly, the wily Daley provided one more display of cleverness. He called upon the city's leading school-reform organization, the Citizens' Schools Committee, to develop a plan for reconstituting the screening commission, which, as the mayor put it, had become "too cumbersome."

According to one interpretation of the reconstitution, the new screening commission was more strongly reform-oriented than its predecessor.[14] It certainly appeared that way in a number of respects. First of all, Daley accepted in its entirety the Citizens' Schools Committee's proposal for a new commission.[15] Moreover, the new head of the revised commission was none other than the dean of the University of Chicago School of Education. Finally, the internal nominating procedures of the commission were strengthened by the introduction of a detailed questionnaire for prospective nominees and clear guidelines for making selections.

On the other hand, the votes for reform simply were not there. Both the membership and the behavior of the new commission make this clear. The new commission was composed of thirteen members, ten of whom were to be designated by various civic organizations, while the mayor was given a free hand in selecting the remaining three members. Half of the ten civic organizations served on a permanent basis, and the other half rotated. Of the five permanent members, two were dependable allies of the political organization: the Chicago Federation of Labor and the Association of Commerce and Industry.[16]

Consequently, the mayor was provided with a standing bloc of five certain votes on the thirteen-member commission. In order to acquire a majority vote for his candidates, the mayor only had to influence two of the commission's eight remaining members. This of course does not guarantee political success. Yet in a city as politically well articulated as Chicago, the probability that the mayor would be able to pick up the additional two votes certainly approaches certainty.

The most compelling argument against the increased reform orientation of the new screening commission is, however, its behavior. On two occasions the new commission has gone out of its way, as well as beyond its rules, to accommodate the politicians' interests. On two other occasions, the commission has presented nominees to the mayor who, immediately upon appointment to the school board, cast the deciding vote thwarting a takeover of the board presidency by a reform coalition.

The commission's first extraordinary accommodation occurred when instead of sending the mayor three nominees for a vacancy, as required by the commission's guidelines, the commission elected to send only one name for each of the two vacancies which existed in 1972.[17] The basis for the commission's decision to violate its own policy clearly appears to have been politically motivated. One of the nominees sent to the mayor was the school board's perennial chairman of the collective-bargaining subcommittee, Marge Wild, an ardent admirer and close supporter of Mayor Daley's views. The other uncontested nominee, Bernard Friedman, while manifesting reform behavior on some issues, also was a consistent supporter of the contract settlements with the teachers' union.

The new commission violated its internal policy the following year, again in order to accommodate the politicians' interests. The procedure established by the commission to designate a nominee is to vote on all of the applicants coming before the commission. The three individuals receiving the greatest number of votes then become the candidates who are recommended to the mayor. However, in 1973 the commission ran into grave difficulty as a result of this procedure. By tradition, organized labor retains two seats on the school board, labor being a close ally of the political organization. The candidate sent to the commission by organized labor this time, though, was unable to muster a sufficient number of votes to qualify as one of the commission's top three candidates.[18]

Consequently, the commission was left in the difficult political situation of having three nominees for the mayor, none of whom was affiliated with organized labor. The commission elected to resolve its problem in a decidedly unreformed manner. The merit-based criteria for selecting candidates were temporarily suspended in favor of using political tradition to designate one of the 1973 candidates. Needless to say, the mayor sided with the commission's exceptional criterion, and promptly selected the labor candidate from among the three nominees sent over by the commission.

On two occasions, the commission also has sent over recommended appointments to the mayor who proved to be the deciding votes against an imminent takeover of the school board presidency by reform-oriented board members. The first time this occurred the commission members claimed to have been unaware that an impending reformer coup was on. The second time, however, everyone in the city knew. Yet the commission still wound up sending the mayor a nominee who voted with the political organization's faction against the reformers' presidential candidate.[19]

Thus, it can be seen that since 1946 the screening commission has moved through three phases. At the outset the commission displayed a reform orientation, placing a majority of reformers on the board. Then the commission adopted an even-handed role, dividing its recommendations between reform- and machine-oriented nominees. Yet the commission was still willing to challenge the mayor, as in 1968 when it refused to recommend two of the mayor's close allies for reappointment. However, with the reconstitution of the screening commission in 1969, the commission no longer appears to possess much of a reform orientation, nor is it any longer inclined to challenge the mayor.

School Board Officers

The three phases through which school board member selection passed might be considered as forms of political independence, accommodation, and subjugation. The election of school board officers follows a similar pattern, and there is a common basis for the similarity. Political incentives determine the extent of involvement in the schools by the political organization. Thus, during nearly the first two decades following the reform of the schools in 1946, a time when few political incentives existed in the city's schools, reformers occupied the school board presidency. However, the schools' civil-rights problems dramatically altered the politicians' view of the schools. Accordingly, in 1964 a school board member closely allied with the political organization was elected president. Subsequently, after collective bargaining had become the schools' primary political problem, one of organized labor's representatives on the school board was elected president in 1970.

Actually, the reformers lost their voting majority on the school board some time before they lost the presidency. William Traynor, the first blue-ribbon reformer to occupy the presidency, usually was able to count on a slim 6–5 vote to sustain his views, as well as those of Superintendent Herold Hunt, whom Traynor solidly supported. However, by the time Claire Roddewig, another blue-ribbon reformer, was elected to the board presidency in 1962, only three or four votes could typically be produced for reformist proposals. Racial discrimination had become the central issue by then. Thus, while Roddewig favored integration, he was overwhelmed by the opposition of the political organization's allies on the board and by Superintendent Willis.[20]

Following Roddewig's resignation in 1964, the board elected to remove much of the tension on the board by selecting as its new president a man who was a strong supporter of Mayor Daley and a solid supporter of Superintendent Willis's segregationist "neighborhood schools" policy. The vice-presidency remained, as before, in the hands of one of organized labor's representatives on the board. Thus, in spite of the advisory screening commission and the importation of nationally renowned superintendents, the schools became solidly reconnected to the city's politics with the election of school board officers in 1964.[21]

Essential but risky maneuvering by Mayor Daley in 1968, however, very nearly severed the political organization's principal tie to the schools. In that year the advisory screening commission failed to recommend for reappointment either the president or the vice-president of the board. Daley overrode the commission on both appointments, but in order to appease the outraged reformers and blacks, he nearly tipped the balance on the board back in favor of the reformers. Daley appointed a third black to the board, added another reformer, and reappointed the board's leading reformer, Warren Bacon, a black businessman. The wheeling and dealing did get the mayor past the main problem of reappointing his political allies with a minimum of damage. However, it also set the stage for a reformer to run for the school board presidency.

The very next year the first signs of trouble appeared. The incumbent board president, Frank Whiston, was forced for the first time to cast a vote for himself in order to gain the six votes required for reelection.[22] The close vote indicated the reformers' growing dissatisfaction with Whiston, and that the reformers were only one vote short of removing the source of their unhappiness. Consequently, Mayor Daley would have to carefully review the recommendations of the screening commission in order to retain his ally in the presidency.

All of the miscalculations, however, were made by the screening commission. In spite of two close calls, the political organization never did lose control of the school board presidency. The first close call occurred in the next election of school board officers, in 1970. The reformers on the board surreptitiously had decided to seek the presidency. The basis for their secrecy was that the reformers' presidential candidate was up for reappointment prior to the election; therefore, everything hinged upon Daley being kept unaware. As it turned out, the plan remained so secret that even the screening commission members were kept unaware. Therefore, the commission sent over the reformer to the mayor, along with two other nominees, one of whom had solid political credentials. Evidently, though, the mayor discovered the reformers' plot. For he dropped his policy of reappointing any board member seeking retention in order to appoint the politically well-connected candidate in the reformers' place.[23] Thus, the reformers' coup died aborning.

The second close call occurred the same year. Shortly after being reelected, both the president and the vice-president died.[24] As a result, a special election had to be called. For this election the reformers openly acknowledged their intention to seek the board presidency. Nevertheless, the results were the same. The reformers were one vote short of a majority, so the key to a reformer victory was of course the voter replacing the president. This time, well aware of the reformers' intentions, the advisory screening commission seemed to openly side with the school board's reform faction. The commission sent the mayor three recommendations, all of whom appeared to be solid reformers: a prominent banker with a long list of civic involvements, a candidate sponsored by the reformist Citizens' Schools Committee, and a candidate backed by the liberal League of Women Voters. The mayor selected the League of Women Voter's candidate, and at her first board meeting she cast the deciding vote for the political organization's presidential candidate.[25]

Following that close call, the political organization's allies on the board proceeded to put an end to the reformers' aspirations for the presidency. For the vice-presidency, the machine faction supported a black woman, Carey Preston, who was a member of the reform faction. Preston's acceptance of the nomination provided the machine faction with virtual assurance that the reform faction's presidential candidate, the black businessman Warren Bacon, would no longer be an acceptable prospect. Reform is one thing, two blacks at the top is something else, and there were racial tensions among the reform faction. The evidence from the next presidential election confirms the soundness of the machine faction's strategy. The machine's candidate was uncontested, and he received a unanimous vote.[26]

In addition to the president's considerable influence over the day-to-day affairs of the schools, a primary reason that the political organization places a great deal of value on the school board presidency involves the president's appointive powers. Of critical importance since the advent of collective bargaining with the teachers are the president's collective-bargaining committee appointments. In this regard, the political organization's interests have been well served by the board presidents. In terms of membership on the three-member committee, at least two seats always have been held by members of the machine faction. Organized labor usually has occupied one of the positions as well. Finally, the chairman of the committee since 1967 has been Marge Wild, regarded by many observers as the mayor's most loyal school board ally. In terms of the way committee members have voted on the collective-bargaining settlements with the teachers, a clear bias is no less apparent. Of the eight members who have served on the committee since 1966, five had a perfect record of support for the settlements. Indeed, only one committee member, Warren Bacon, the leader of the board's reform faction, has voted favorably for the settlements less than 60 percent of the time. Table 5-1 illustrates the composition and collective-bargaining voting behavior of the committee.

Table 5-1
Collective Bargaining Committee: Chicago Board of Education, 1966-1978

Date of Appointment	Membership	Affiliation	Percentage of favorable votes (number of votes)
1966	Edward Scheffler	former judge	100% (1)
	Thomas Murray	organized labor	100% (4)
	Marge Wild	socialite	100% (10)
1967	(As above except that Wild served as chairman.)		
1968	Marge Wild		
	Thomas Murray		
	John Carey	organized labor	100% (11)
1969	Marge Wild		
	Thomas Murray		
	Carey Preston	Urban League	60% (10)
1971 (April)	Marge Wild		
	Carey Preston		
	Gerald Sbarboro	staff attorney for Democratic officials	80% (5)[a]
1971 (August)	Marge Wild		
	Gerald Sbarboro		
	Warren Bacon	businessman	17% (7)
1974	Marge Wild		
	Carey Preston		
	Thomas Nayder	organized labor	100% (7)

Source: Proceedings of the Chicago Board of Education.

[a]Sbarboro opposed the two-year agreement signed in 1971 on the grounds that a multiyear contract was illegal. He did not, however, express any opposition to the substantive terms of the settlement. In effect, Sbarboro, as with all of the machine's faction who served on the committee, is a 100% supporter of the settlements with the teachers' union.

The School Superintendency

It is not necessary to dwell at any length on the superintendency channel of influence, since the topic already has received our consideration. The central point is that the pattern of political activity involving the superintendent is similar to the pattern of activity we have observed at two other channels of access. During each of the three different forms of urban governance there have been significantly varying amounts of political incentive in the schools. Corresponding to the amount of incentive, the superintendency has varied in the degree to which the politicians have exerted influence on the office holder. Since 1936, the city's public schools have had five superintendents, and, as we shall see, each had a distinctively different relationship to the political organization.

The machine-rule superintendent, William Johnson, was purely and simply an agent of the political organization. During Johnson's tenure as superintendent (1936–1946), the schools functioned as though they were up for sale to the highest bidder, and from his vantage point as superintendent, Johnson even submitted a bid or two of his own. Textbooks authored by the superintendent were required reading in the schools, for which he of course received royalties. Johnson also ran a training class for prospective school principals, and a suspiciously high percentage of his students eventually became principals.[27] As the accreditation scandal ultimately revealed, the city's schools reached their lowest level under the extraordinary stewardship of William Johnson.

Once the schools came under reform rule, as a result of the accreditation scandal, Johnson's reign as superintendent was over. Indeed, the political organization's leadership was so exceedingly anxious to separate itself from the scandal-infested schools that it allowed itself to become convinced that the schools had to be turned over to the reformers. Accordingly, a series of superintendents who had no ties to the political organization whatsoever came in to head the city's schools. Under reform rule it even became a matter of prudent tradition to recruit superintendents from well beyond the bounds of the city in order to avoid any appearance of political contamination.

The first reform superintendent, Herold Hunt, immediately proved his reform intentions by abolishing virtually all school patronage, and the reform-oriented school board followed suit by eliminating spoils as a consideration in dispensing school contracts and other valuable benefits. Hunt's two great advantages were that he had the political organization's reform-oriented front man, Martin Kennelly, serving as mayor, and he had the nearness of the scandal to protect him against any designs of the party to return the schools to a policy of business as usual.

Superintendent Hunt's successor, Benjamin Willis, lacked both of these advantages; however, he possessed two other advantages of his own. Without patronage and spoils, the school system had become to a considerable degree politically irrelevant. Superintendent Willis also had solid business-community backing and a forceful personality that brooked no opposition, even from school board members. Hence, what might have been a perilous transition was made with ease, and under Willis the city's schools became more reformed than ever before.

Willis's problems began when the schools became no longer politically irrelevant. As soon as the civil-rights problems in the schools spilled over into the city's politics, the political organization breached the reform barriers surrounding the schools with remarkable ease. Willis was quietly replaced by still another blue-ribbon reformer from outside the city, James Redmond.

Hunt and Willis each had certain critical advantages in their favor, then, in establishing reform rule in the schools: for Hunt there was the immediacy of the accreditation scandal, a reform-oriented mayor, and a supportive school board, while Willis had a dominating personality, a mayor anxious to establish himself among the city's reform and business interests, and a school system possessed of few political incentives to cause intervention by the party. Redmond, on the other hand, possessed none of these advantages and few others besides. By the time Redmond succeeded to the superintendency, the schools had become a political hot spot; the school board had come under the sway of the political organization's allies on the board; and Daley had far more leeway to involve himself in the schools, having firmly established himself with the city's business interests. To make matters even more difficult, Redmond had none of Willis's tenacity, preferring instead to capitulate and avoid conflict whenever the board showed any reluctance to follow his leadership.

Thus, while Redmond came out of the same reform tradition as Hunt and Willis, the schools no longer offered the same opportunity to pursue a reform strategy. Redmond nevertheless attempted to achieve a number of reform objectives, notably the racial integration of the city's schools. Redmond also attempted to maintain himself, in Paul Peterson's words, "as the leader of a united educational community, who had to protect the interests of his professional associates vis-à-vis outsiders," a characteristic reform attitude.[28] Consequently, while the Redmond administration possessed several outward signs of reform, the city's schools in fact were no longer nearly as reformed as they had been. The political obstacles to reform simply had become too formidable.

The chief political obstacle to maintaining the schools as a relatively autonomous reform enterprise, once the furor surrounding the racial-integration issue had subsided, was collective bargaining. The institutionalization of setting labor interests against management interests by its very nature made Redmond's commitment to avoid conflict and maintain the appearance of unity obsolete as a managerial strategy. Then, when the leadership of the teachers' union changed hands in 1972 and the union began to pursue a much more militant and independent course of action, it became evident that the strategy also had become politically dysfunctional.[29]

The political organization responded to Redmond's obsolescence by approving the school board's hiring of an entirely different type of superintendent. Redmond's successor, Joseph Hannon, as we have said, may be distinguished from his reform-rule predecessors both politically and managerially. Hunt, Willis, and Redmond had all served as superintendents of other major school systems before coming to Chicago, and all three men were highly esteemed by their educational colleagues. Hannon, on the other hand, was recruited from within the Chicago system, where he had been serving in the educationally peripheral area of facilities planning.[30] Hannon also has had no experience as a superintendent elsewhere. Thus, Hannon's standing among educators is significantly lower than his predecessors. In turn, Hannon's loyalties are far more likely to be with those to whom he is beholden for creating his career, namely the leadership of the political organization.

Once Hannon began his superintendency, a second major difference emerged. Hannon's reform-rule predecessors had identified the fundamental source of conflict in school politics as being external to the school system, namely the political organization. The basic conflict was the professional schoolmen versus the partisan politicians. In contrast, Hannon has identified the conflict as internal. For Hannon, the basic threat to the school system comes from the teachers, who have so leveled the school system through collective bargaining that very little managerial control or teacher accountability remains.[31] Thus, Hannon's designation as superintendent is simply additional evidence of the extent to which union rule has replaced reform rule in the schools.

Hannon's superintendency also can be viewed as the extent to which the political organization has penetrated the schools. On the one hand, Hannon's efforts to reduce the power and influence of the teachers' union in the schools reflects the political organization's growing disenchantment with the teachers. Hannon also has come to the aid of the political organization much more directly. The extent to which the new superintendent is willing to use his position to accommodate the party is well revealed by his behavior during the special mayoral election following Daley's death. To replace Daley the party slated an obscure and lackluster candidate, Michael Bilandic, which presented the party with a serious name-recognition problem. Doing his share for the cause, Hannon resurrected a practice which had not been used in the schools since the heyday of machine rule. One week prior to the election, the superintendent authorized the distribution of a pamphlet through all of the city's schools that contained notable accomplishments and facts about the city. Featured on the cover of the pamphlet was none other than the party's candidate for mayor, the justification being that the candidate was serving as the acting mayor.[32] Decorously, the pamphlet did not provide the voters with the candidate's voting machine lever number.

School Board Members

Two important observations can be made about political influence upon the school board members as a whole. To begin with, the level of political activity here follows the same general pattern that we have observed at the other three channels of influence into the school policy-formation process. Following the reform of the schools in 1946, reform-oriented board members occupied a majority of the seats on the board, and the politicians exerted infrequent influence on the members. This may be said to signify a period of political independence. However, as political incentives reemerged in the schools during the 1960s, the number of school board members that the political organization was able to influence correspondingly increased. Thus, as we shall see shortly, by the time collective bargaining began in 1967, the political organization's allies constituted a majority of the school board's membership. Nevertheless, there was at the same time a significant faction of reform-oriented board members who vigorously opposed the political party's allies on a number of issues. Consequently, this period may be considered as one of political accommodation. In contrast, after the mayor made several new appointments in 1974, a significant reform coalition no longer existed on the board. The school board's leading reformer, the black businessman Warren Bacon, was replaced, as was Maria Cerda, another outspoken critic of the political organization's faction on the board. Significantly, Bacon and Cerda were the two board members who most consistently had opposed the school board's settlements with the teacher's union.[33] Thus, the current school board politics may be regarded as a period of political subjugation.

The other important observation to be made about political influence upon the school board is that while it follows the general pattern of political influence on the schools, it is in another respect unique. At all three of the other channels of access, the influence exerted by the political organization is typically indirect: the influence is exerted by intermediaries. This enables the politicians and the schoolmen to maintain that the city's schools operate independently of the city's politics—an important consideration for the political organization because of the strong and widespread public support for maintaining an autonomous school system.

Yet, when it comes to exerting influence on the school board as a whole in regard to collective bargaining, the mayor frequently has openly and directly involved himself in the process. The means by which the mayor has been able to intervene is by serving as a labor mediator. Apparently, most observers do not regard the mediation role as constituting undue political interference. As it is conventionally understood, mediation only occurs when an impasse has been reached by the negotiating parties. Hence, the role of mediator is imposed upon the mayor, rather than being sought by him. As well, the role is ostensibly neutral. The objective of the mediator is to produce an agreement acceptable to both parties, rather than to benefit one party at the other's expense. Finally, no significant benefits accrue to the mediator as a result of the process; he is simply a go-between.

What is intriguing, however, about Mayor Daley's school mediation, and what makes the open nature of the relationship between Daley and the school board all the more interesting, is that the mediation does not conform to any of the three conventional mediation characteristics just mentioned. As we shall see, it is not at all apparent that the mediation role has been thrust upon, rather than sought, by Mayor Daley. Nor does it appear that the mayor conducted a majority of the mediation sessions in a manner which benefited the school board as well as the teachers. Additionally, it would appear that the mayor himself has been a principal beneficiary of the mediation. Certainly his successful mediation has enhanced his reputation among the general public as an effective administrator. Then, by becoming the effective source of benefits for the teachers, he, rather then the school board, becomes the recipient of the teachers' gratitude.

By examining in detail the voting behavior of the school board members in regard to collective bargaining, the observations we have made can be better appreciated. Listed in table 5-2 is the voting record for each of the school board members who has voted on a collective-bargaining settlement. For the sake of lending greater clarity to the data, board members have been divided into three

Table 5-2
Chicago School Board: Collective Bargaining Voting and Mayoral Participation, 1967–1978

Member	1967	1968	1969	1970	1971	1972	1973	1974	1975	1976	1977	1978	PERCENTAGE PRO-LABOR VOTE
PRO-LABOR BLOC													
Carey	+	+	+	+	+	+	+	A	+	+	+	+	100 %
Murray / Nayder	+	+	+	(vacancy)	Nayder +	+	+	+	+	+	+	+	100
Wild	+	+	+	+	A	+	+	+	+	+	A	+	100
Scheffler / Epps	+	X	X	X	X	X	X	Epps +	+	+	A	A	100
Whiston / Sbarboro / Johnson	+	+	+	−	Sbarboro +	+	+	+	+	Johnson +	+	+	92
Friedman / O'Hern	+	A	A	+	+	+	+	A	−	+	O'Hern +	+	89
Green / Boutte / McGee	−	+	Boutte +	−	+	+	+	McGee +	+	+	A	A	80
Valasquez	X	X	X	X	X	X	X	Valasquez +	−	+	+	+	80
ANTI-LABOR BLOC													
Bacon	+	A	−	−	−	−	−	X	X	X	X	X	17
Cerda	X	X	Cerda X	−	+	−	−	X	X	X	X	X	25
Witkowsky	X	Witkowsky +	−	−	X	X	X	X	X	X	X	X	33
SWING VOTERS													
Adams / Preston	A	Preston +	−	+	+	−	−	+	+	+	A	−	60
Malis	+	+	+	−	+	−	−	+	−	+	A	−	50
Oliver / Rohter	+	+	−	Rohter X	+	A	A	+	−	−	+	A	63
	9-1	9-0	6-4	6-5	7-2	6-4	6-4	9-0	7-4	10-1	6-0	6-2	
MAYORAL PARTICIPATION													
	+	+	+	−	+	−	+	−	+	−	−	−	

+ = YES   A = Absent
− = NO   X = Unoccupied

Sources: The votes were drawn from the <u>Proceedings of the Chicago Board of Education</u>. Mayoral participation was drawn from the <u>Chicago Sun Times</u> and <u>Chicago Tribune</u>.

voting blocs based on their cumulative collective-bargaining voting record. In order to better understand Mayor Daley's role in the settlement process, below each year's settlement vote is an indication of whether or not the mayor participated.

The table amply confirms the extent to which the political organization had regained a substantial measure of influence over school policy making by the mid-1960s. Every one of the school board members that Paul Peterson identified as being a member of the "machine" faction is among the pro-labor voting bloc.[34] The consistency with which pro-labor has remained the majority voting bloc and the consistency with which the bloc has supported the collective-bargaining settlements are nothing short of remarkable. In only one year, 1971, has the pro-labor bloc failed to constitute a majority, and the absence of a majority in 1971 was merely the result of a temporary vacancy, which promptly was filled by a pro-labor appointment. As for voting consistency, of the seventy-two votes cast by the pro-labor bloc, only five have been negative, and, at that, one of the five was only a technical objection against the signing of a patently illegal multiyear contract in 1971.

In contrast, the group of board members which Paul Peterson identified as the "reform" faction displays no such unity, dominance, or voting consistency. The fact that the reformers on the board have not consistently opposed the collective-bargaining settlements is an important consideration. One of the chief characteristics Peterson used to distinguish reformers from machine allies was their opposition to collective bargaining and the deficit budgeting that resulted from the collective-bargaining settlements. Nevertheless, the reformers are all over the board on the issue. One of the reformers, Bernard Friedman, is even among the pro-labor bloc. Friedman registered only one negative vote, and that occurred in 1975, the year in which Mayor Daley disrupted a social gathering of the school board in order to dictate the terms of a settlement which was highly favorable to the teachers.[35] The other reformers split along anti-labor and swing-vote lines, with the swing voters representing a majority.

Given the inconsistency of the reformers' opposition to the settlements as a whole, when the swing voters' behavior is examined more closely some consistency can be identified. The swing voters went through two clear shifts in their views toward the collective-bargaining settlements. During the first two negotiations, they provided complete support for the two settlements mediated by Daley. However, after that the swing voters turned against the union, regardless of Daley's participation. With the exception of 1971, a year in which the settlement solution of a multiyear contract was proposed by the board's leading reformer, Warren Bacon, between 1969 and 1973 the swing bloc cast only two of its ten votes in favor of the settlements. Then, from 1974 onward the swing bloc voted as real swingers, casting 58 percent of its twelve votes positively.

What is interesting about the shifts in the behavior of the swing voters is that these shifts would appear to have more to do with politics than the substance of the contracts. With one exception, all of the contracts agreed to by the school board have entailed deficits and substantial benefit increases for the teachers at the expense of benefits which would have more directly benefited the schools' students. However, when Daley mediated the first two agreements, he agreed to seek the funds needed to make up the deficit. As it turned out, though, the mayor was only partially successful in 1968, thereby leaving the school board with its first genuine deficit. Consequently, when in 1969 the mayor once again agreed to seek the money required to finance still another deficit budget, only one of the swing voters was persuaded to go along.[36]

The second shift was produced by even more direct political means. In 1974 the mayor replaced the two members making up the small anti-labor bloc, Bacon and Cerda, with two appointees, Epps and Valasquez, who had far more positive attitudes toward the aspirations of the unionized teachers. A third appointment, the replacement of the occasional reformer Boutte by the elderly ex-postmaster McGee, clearly signaled an end to whatever hopes the reformers may have harbored toward becoming a significant factor in the board's labor negotiations with the teachers' union. It has become clear that voting against the settlements is a futile, lonely, and even dangerous action, if a board member had any intentions of serving more than a single term.[37]

What is particularly significant about the composition and collective-bargaining voting behavior of the board is that it brings into serious question the basis for Mayor Daley's frequent participation in the settlement process. The data clearly reveal that the mayor consistently has had a majority bloc of allies on the board, and that his allies almost invariable have supported the settlements with the teachers' union—regardless of the terms of the agreements and whether or not the mayor mediated the settlement. Moreover, there are a number of indirect means the mayor could have used to influence school board member behavior short of formal mediation. Finally, the reformers on the board hardly appear to be a very formidable opposition, and on several occasions they have voted favorably on settlements without the mayor's formal intervention. Nevertheless, in a majority of instances (six of the ten settlements), Mayor Daley openly intervened in the settlement process.

What the data therefore strongly indicate is that Mayor Daley, rather than either of the negotiating parties, may well have initiated his participation. This interpretation can be better appreciated by distinguishing between conventional and political types of mediation. As we have said, conventional mediation is imposed by the negotiating parties on the mediator. The mediator performs in a neutral manner, favoring neither party. A conventional mediator also acquires no significant benefits as a result of his mediation; only the negotiating parties benefit.

Political mediation is altogether different. A political mediator, being a politician, must include calculations concerning his own advantage in the mediation process. Indeed, a first order of business for a political mediator is to make certain that he possesses the means to produce a settlement, regardless of its terms. For electoral and other political judgments will be based in part upon how effectively a politician is able to resolve a labor dispute, particularly in an area as emotionally significant as the schools.

From this point of view, then, it is not remarkable that Mayor Daley may have initiated some of the calls for mediation while knowing full well that a majority of the school board members were prepared to vote favorably on a settlement without the necessity of mediation. In this way the mayor could conduct the mediation in what would appear to be a highly expeditious manner, for which he then would receive the favorable political judgments sought by a political mediator.

Of course, since mediation involves two parties, this type of arrangement was more likely to have obtained during the early, moderate years of union rule. During this period, the mayor was able to exert considerable influence on the union leadership as well as on a majority of the school board members. Accordingly, three of the four mediation sessions conducted by Daley during the moderate union-rule period required only a single day in which to produce an agreement. [38]

In turn, once the more militant and independent leadership took over the union, Daley's mediation was not so easily accomplished. Following the lengthy 1973 strike, it took the mayor three days to bring about an agreement, and Daley had to resort to threatening board members in order to produce a bare majority agreement. The union leadership was simply unwilling to make any compromise, and even some of the mayor's allies on the board balked at being asked to accept such unusual terms.[39] Indeed, the 1973 agreement is one of only two agreements for which none of the swing voters was willing to cast a favorable vote. The pro-labor orientation of all three of the replacements Daley made on the school board the following year may be explained in large part by the difficulty the mayor experienced during the 1973 mediation session. The difficulty in 1973 may also explain why the mayor elected to forego mediation in the 1975 strike in favor of simply disrupting a board gathering in order to demand a settlement which was highly favorable to the union. Mayor Daley's extraordinary behavior reflects the extent to which negotiations and the mayor's role in them had dramatically changed under the fully developed form of union rule.

The mayor's mediation also violated the neutrality principle of conventional mediation. Once again, his behavior is understandable when the mediation process is viewed as a political activity in which the mayor is a principal beneficiary, rather than simply a disinterested go-between. A political mediator usually cannot allow himself to be bound by the assumptions that equity is a desirable outcome and that equity can be achieved by treating facts in a detached, even-handed manner. Political mediation involves a substantial amount of what Max Weber referred to as "kadi" justice and a good deal of downright bias.

The extent to which the mayor favored the union's demands over those of the school board can be seen by making a simple comparison: the board's increasing budgetary deficits versus the teachers' broad and substantial range of benefit increases. Again, however, a distinction must be drawn between the imbalance which occurred during the period of moderate union rule as opposed to the period of fully developed union rule. During the early negotiations, the increases generally were kept within the bounds of resources available to the board. After Daley had failed to secure enough funds to cover the 1968 deficit, the union leadership's demands of the school board became more modest. However, there were other elements in the union who preferred a more independent and aggressive course, which forced a more militant course of action than the leadership preferred. Nevertheless, after negotiating four contracts with the union, the school board was able to announce when entering the 1971 negotiations that there was no deficit.[40]

That, as it turned out, was the last time the school board was able to make such a claim. As a result of the 1971 contract, the board in 1972 said it faced a $100 million deficit. The board also said, however, that a clause in the contract allowed the board to withhold the benefit increases that had been negotiated for 1972 because of the deficit. The clause in turn proved to be the downfall of the union's moderate leadership. With the rise of the union's new leadership in 1972, the board's deficit has risen as well. While it is difficult to judge from the information contained in the board's massive and complex budget, the deficit apparently never dipped below $70 million after 1971, and by 1978 the deficit was estimated at nearly $90 million.[41] What the union has done to increase the board's deficit, as we have seen, is to present a list of demands and then wait for the board, the mayor, or both to finally capitulate. Thus, under fully developed union rule, the entire bargaining process, including the mayor's mediation, is much more sharply biased in the union's favor.

It is easy enough to see how a political mediator benefits from the mediation process. One of the two principal objectives a political mediator seeks to acquire through the mediation process is to become perceived by the benefiting parties as the source of their benefits. In this way, he becomes the recipient of their gratitude. Thus, unlike conventional mediation, political mediation involves a reciprocal relationship between the mediator and the negotiating parties. In the instance that we have examined, the reciprocity exists between Mayor Daley and the teachers' union. The school board, after all, has far fewer benefits which it can offer the mayor in exchange for his assistance, and the board is, in any event, well populated by the Mayor's political allies.

A successful political mediator acquires his other primary benefit from the public. From the public's point of view, mediation's principal objective is the maintenance or restoration of public order. Thus, successful mediation is more concerned with producing an expeditious settlement than one which is equitable or financially sound. The manner in which the media treat mediation would appear to be largely responsible for the manner in which it is handled by political mediators. Budgets are complex documents and budgetary procedures are flexible instruments. As well, the financial consequences of a settlement do not occur immediately. Thus, the media dwell on the issue of order, and the issue of cost is regarded more casually. However, there are limits to the extent that politicians can slight the cost factor, as developments in New York City have amply demonstrated.

Thus, it appears that brief and controlled public disorders can actually work to the politicians' advantage, and for this reason the politicians may be viewed as having an interest in bringing about this form of disorder. Employing such a strategy is of course contingent upon a politician's reasonable expectation that the means are at hand to terminate the disorder. Such is one of the means by which a city's administration is then enabled to publicly proclaim that it governs a "city that works," even when the city's less public financial and achievement records surely indicate that the much-vaunted stability is being achieved at costs which are well out of line with the benefits, and which may eventually make the city unworkable except for those who work it.

Notes

1. Paul E. Peterson, "The Politics of American Education," in Fred Kerlinger and John Carroll, eds., *Review of Research in Education.* Vol. II (Itasca, Ill.: Peacock, 1974).

2. Alan Rosenthal, *Pedagogues and Power: Teacher Groups in School Politics* (Syracuse, N.Y.: Syracuse University Press, 1969), p. 151.

3. Robert Crain and James Vanecko, "Elite Influence in School Desgregation," in James Q. Wilson, ed., *City Politics and Public Policy* (New York: John Wiley and Sons, 1968).

4. Edward Banfield, *Political Influence* (New York: Free Press, 1961). Robert Dahl, *Who Governs* (New Haven, Conn.: Yale University Press, 1961).

5. A more general point of view along such lines is provided by Peter Bachrach and Morton Baratz, "Two Faces of Power," *American Political Science Review* 57 (December 1962), pp. 947-952.

6. An extreme instance is contained in Joseph Pois's account of the Willis administration. Pois served as a school board member during part of the Willis superintendency. See *The School Board Crisis: A Chicago Case Study* (Chicago: Educational Methods, 1964).

7. Compliance relationships have been well analyzed by the sociologist Amitai W. Etzioni, *A Comparative Analysis of Complex Organizations* (New York: Free Press, 1961).

8. Paul Peterson's analysis of Chicago school politics contains an interesting treatment of the ideological nature of much of school politics. See *School Politics: Chicago Style* (Chicago: University of Chicago Press, 1976), especially pp. 56-78.

9. Ibid., p. 104.

10. Mary J. Herrick, *The Chicago Schools: A Social and Political History* (Beverly Hills, Cal.: Sage Publications, 1971).

11. Ibid., pp. 274-275.

12. Peterson, *School Politics*, p. 94.

13. According to a newspaper account, the vote was 9-8. Cited and discussed in Peterson, *School Politics*, p. 97.

14. Ibid., pp. 103-106.

15. Mayor Daley's press release and the proposal submitted to the mayor are on file with the Citizens' Schools Committee. Both documents recommend an identical composition for the advisory commission.

16. The other three permanent members are the Citizens' Schools Committee, the PTA, and the Urban League. All three organizations would likely appoint reform-oriented representatives to the commission. However, both the PTA and the Urban League have representatives on the school board, Louise Malis and Carey Preston respectively, who do not vote strictly along reform lines. Their voting record on collective bargaining is analyzed later in the chapter.

17. The commission's guidelines state that the "Commission shall submit and publish the names of at least three qualified persons for each vacancy to be filled, even in cases where incumbent board members have indicated a desire for reappointment." Citizens' Schools Committee, press release, May 10, 1972.

18. Mayor's Advisory Commission on School Board Nominees, minutes of meeting, July 9, 1973. According to the minutes, the labor candidate, Thomas Nayder, received only three votes from an eleven-member interviewing committee.

19. Both of the events are further discussed shortly.

20. Herrick, *Chicago Schools*, pp. 314-316.

21. The close political and labor ties of the new school board president, Frank Whiston, are described in Peterson, *School Politics*, pp. 18, 26.

22. *Proceedings of the Chicago Board of Education*, May 28, 1969.

23. Ibid., May 27, 1970. After the mayor appointed Gerald Sbarboro in place of Jack Witkowsky, the reformers did not contest the incumbent board officers. The vote for the incumbent president was 6-2 with three abstentions.

24. Both men were over seventy years of age.

25. *Proceedings*, December 31, 1970. The vote featured the school board's first secret election and the meeting was held on New Year's Eve. Nevertheless,

it is a virtual certainty that the new board member, Katherine Rohter, voted for the party's candidate, since the board had been deadlocked up to the time of her appointment.

26. Ibid., July 28, 1971.

27. Herrick, *Chicago Schools*, pp. 237, 247.

28. Peterson, *School Politics*, p. 201.

29. Redmond did come around gradually to an awareness of the conflict inherent in collective bargaining with the teachers. Thus, whereas he could contend that the union's 1969 demands represented "not a collective bargaining crisis, it's a crisis of support for the common schools," in the next year Redmond characterized the union's demands as "in excess of reasonable expectations since it results in a tremendous deficit." Both quotes are contained in Peterson, *School Politics*, p. 202. However Redmond apparently remained sympathetic to the unionized teachers to the bitter end. When the school board was considering renewing Redmond's contract for an additional four-year term, the president of the Chicago Teachers' Union publicly urged the school board to retain Redmond, which well may have been a factor in the board's decision to not renew Redmond's contract. *Chicago Tribune*, October 12, 1974.

30. Actually, Redmond had prior experience in the Chicago school system as an aide to Superintendent Hunt. Thus, he was not entirely an outsider.

31. In Hannon's words, "We are starting to put more accountability into our schools; but due process—it's killing us. It's a constraint." *Chicago Daily News*, April 6, 1977.

32. Distribution of the pamphlet was reported in a local CBS-TV news commentary during the week preceding the special mayoral election.

33. Table 5-2 provides data on board member voting behavior in regard to the collective-bargaining settlements.

34. Paul Peterson used several criteria to distinguish "machine" and "reform" factions on the Chicago school board, among them voting behavior on the collective-bargaining settlements. According to Peterson's analysis, the union supporters were Whiston, Carey, Nayder, Green, Boutte, Sbarboro, Wild, and Murray. The union opponents were Preston, Adams, Bacon, Oliver, Malis, Witkowsky, Cerda, and Rohter. Friedman is classified as a swing voter. Accordingly, regard for the union falls right along the machine–reform axis. See Peterson, *School Politics*, pp. 189, 283.

35. Peterson's analysis shows Friedman voting against the settlements more often than is indicated by the school board's minutes. Apparently, Peterson relied on newspaper accounts of the voting that took place in Mayor Daley's office during mediation, in which case either the newspapers were in error or Friedman subsequently changed his mind. In general, our analysis does not show the reformers to be as strongly opposed to the teachers' union as Peterson's study indicates. See his "The Politics of Collective Bargaining," chapter 8 in *School Politics*.

36. Bacon, Witkowsky, and Oliver all expressed concern that the board should not enter into an agreement involving benefit increases unless it was made contingent upon the availability of funds. *Proceedings*, May 25, 1969.

37. As table 5–2 indicates, only Bacon among the three board members making up the anti-labor bloc served more than a single term.

38. The exception occurred in 1969 when the union delegates overrode the union leadership's opposition and voted to strike while Mayor Daley was conducting mediation. *Chicago Sun Times*, May 22, 1969.

39. Although the pro-labor bloc shows an overwhelming degree of support for the settlements, some members of the bloc were less closely tied to the political organization than others. Newspaper accounts indicate that the mayor could initially produce only four votes for the proposed settlement. The two holdouts from the pro-labor bloc probably were Friedman and Boutte, both of whom occasionally sided with the reformers; Friedman did so quite frequently in fact. *Chicago Sun Times*, January 24, 1973.

40. *Chicago Sun Times*, January 12, 1971.

41. Newspaper accounts of the school board's deficits vary from report to report. At times a larger deficit is reported before a settlement than after, even though a substantial increase has been negotiated. The reporting in large part simply reflects the school board's own statements about the budget, which vary from day to day. The school board has resorted to so much gimmickry with its budget over the years that an accurate assessment of its deficit may be impossible. Thus, in 1976 the deficit was reported being in the neighborhood of $133–$150 million. *Chicago Sun Times*, September 1, 1976.

6 Conclusion

The Union-Rule Model

At the outset, the proposition was presented that unionized employees in the big cities were beginning to play an unprecedented and highly influential role in the governance process. The proposition was specified in greater detail by the development of a model of a union-rule form of government and models of the two preceding major forms of urban governance, machine rule and reform rule respectively. Distinctions among the three models were made along the dimensions of structure, process, and set of actors.

A union-rule form of government is characterized by a high degree of intra-institutional disarticulation of the bureaucratic authority structure. The high degree of interinstitutional disarticulation which characterizes a reform rule also is present in a union-rule form of big-city government. However, a reform-rule governmental structure displays a higher degree of articulation within the bureaucratic authority structure. By contrast, a machine-rule form of government is characterized by a high degree of articulation both within the bureaucracies and among the institutions of government.

Along the dimension of process, a union-rule form of big-city government can be distinguished from a reform-rule form of government by the higher degree of self-interest which characterizes the behavior and objectives of the union rule bureaucrats. Management dominates the bureaucracy under reform rule, and its leadership position in the organization is legitimized by its commitment to serve primarily the interests of the clientele of the organization. Under union rule, the union dominates the bureaucracy, and its leadership position is legitimized by its commitment to serve primarily the interests of the union's membership. In this regard, union rule is similar to machine rule, for the political party of machine rule also is a high-self-interest form of organization. Thus, the political party characteristically uses the public bureaucracies to serve primarily the interests of the party.

The set of actors typically found within a union-rule form of bureaucracy also differs significantly from its reform-rule counterparts, while sharing a number of similarities with the machine-rule bureaucrats. In contrast to reform-rule bureaucrats, union-rule bureaucrats are characteristically more partisan politically, committed to more than simply a particular functional affiliation, and more inclined to regard unilateral managerial influence as illegitimate. The machine-rule bureaucrats also are typically of a highly partisan nature, although in this regard they usually were required to be because of their dependence on the goodwill of the political party for their well-being. Similarly, the machine-rule bureaucrats bear more than a commitment to the particular bureaucracy within which they are employed. They are committed to the political party, just as the union-rule bureaucrat is committed to the union. The machine-rule and union-rule bureaucrats differ, however, in their conception of the legitimacy of unilateral managerial authority and action. The machine-rule bureaucrat accepts the unilateral dictates of management without question.

Testing the Union-Rule Model

It was decided to test the applicability and utility of the union-rule model under an extremely difficult set of circumstances. The rationale for doing so was that if the model held in a situation in which the obstacles were numerous and severe, then the likelihood would be high that the model could be usefully applied to other big cities and other big-city bureaucracies where the obstacles were fewer and less difficult to overcome.

Chicago was selected as the big city in which to test the model for three reasons. To begin with, Chicago in more respects than other big cities still is governed by a powerful political machine. As well, the leadership of the party steadfastly and successfully has opposed granting collective-bargaining rights to the great bulk of the city's employees. Finally, the party leadership has maintained an exceptionally sound financial record compared to most other big cities. Thus, the political party may reasonably be expected to oppose the development of a union-rule form of government for political and financial reasons, and the party possesses a considerable amount of power and influence to support its position.

In order to make the test even more difficult, a highly reformed public bureaucracy was selected for testing the intraorganizational features of the union-rule model: the elementary and secondary school system. A big city's public school bureaucracy invariably is among the most reformed organizations in the city, and, fortunately for our purposes, Chicago's public school system is no exception. Indeed, at the time Chicago's teachers were granted the right to collective bargaining, Chicago's schools were headed by the most powerful and reform-oriented school superintendent in the country, Benjamin Willis. No less than a political party, a highly reformed bureaucracy can reasonably be expected to represent a powerful obstacle to the development of union rule. Union rule's objectives and methods constitute a violation of the principles of reform management and a practical threat to the influence and authority of the managers.

That a higher degree of public concern is directed toward the public schools than toward other public agencies is another factor militating against the development of union rule in the schools. There is strong and widespread public support for the separation of the schools from political influence. While a union is not as politically oriented as a political party, like parties, unions are high-self-interest organizations, unions also engage in highly partisan political activities, and union rule seeks to restructure the schools so that the teachers become the primary beneficiary of the schools.

Finally, the teachers themselves would appear to constitute an impediment to the development of union rule. Teachers are trained in the universities to accept the clientele of the schools as the primary beneficiary, and, as professionals, they are expected to possess a low degree of self-interest. Consequently, the development of a high degree of commitment to a high-self-interest organization such as a union requires a greater reorientation in values and practices for teachers than for other city bureaucrats.

The Applicability of the Union-Rule Model

The extent to which a model "fits" an empirical situation is clearly a cardinal test of the model's value. From this point of view, the data presented in the study may be evaluated in terms of the extent to which they support, modify and also falsify the union-rule model presented in the introductory chapter. After assessing the model in this regard, we shall evaluate the model in terms of its utility, which is to say, for what purposes is the union rule model useful?

The distinguishing structural characteristic of union rule is intrainstitutional disarticulation within an overlay of the interinstitutional disarticulation which distinguished union rule's predecessor, reform rule. If these are read as two propositions, it may be said that the first is confirmed by the data, while the second requires that the model be revised.

As regards the first proposition, we saw particularly in chapter 3 that a considerable and varied amount of disarticulation occurred in the school authority structure following the grant of collective bargaining to the teachers. If many of the items contained in the collective-bargaining contracts reached by the school board and the teachers' union are viewed from a structural standpoint, it can be seen that the teachers have acquired an autonomous and highly authoritative position within the school system. The elaborate procedure dictating the means by which teachers are evaluated, along with the minimal criteria of performance adequacy defined in the contract, virtually assure teachers a permanent position in the schools. The comparative data that were presented on termination serve to indicate just how more secure the union-rule teachers are than their earlier counterparts were under reform and machine rule. The comparative material on the differences in the tenuring procedure also confirms the extent to which union-rule teachers have become virtually free of the dictates of management under which their predecessors were required to work.

We also saw that the union-rule teachers have been able to acquire a broad and significant amount of policy-making authority at every level of the school system. Individual teachers, for example, now possess the authority to determine which students in their classroom will continue to receive instruction. Those conforming to the teacher's behavioral standards are allowed to remain, while those who are not in conformity may be dismissed at the sole discretion of the teacher. At the school level, the contract calls for regular meetings between the principal and the union's Professional Problems Committee. At the school-system level, the union leadership meets regularly with the superintendent and his staff, while joint committees consisting of union and school board members deliberate and set policy in a wide variety of so-called educational areas.

Interestingly enough, however, the overlay of interinstitutional disarticulation which we postulated would carry over from the preceding period of reform rule is not confirmed by the data. Thus, we saw that since the inception of union rule in the schools, and far more since the union leadership changed hands in 1972, the leadership of the political party has made a variety of efforts to regain a strong degree of influence over the schools. By contrast, during the preceding reform-rule period, the party made little effort to influence the schools, being content to allow them to function as an autonomous organization controlled by the professional management for the most part, particularly during the administration of the autocratic Superintendent Willis.

Thus, we saw that at all four of the major access points into the school policy-formation process, the same general pattern occurred. During the machine-rule period, the political party penetrated all four access channels and thoroughly dominated the school policy-formation process. Then with the advent of reform rule, the party lost virtually all of its access into the schools. Nationally renowned superintendents were recruited from outside the city, reformers dominated the school board and occupied the chief board offices, and even the mayor's authority to appoint members to the school board was sharply circumscribed. Nevertheless, once union rule began to develop in the schools, the data clearly indicate that the political party was once again able to penetrate all four of the school system's principal points of access into the policy-formation process.

Yet, the data also clearly indicate that despite the efforts and considerable influence of the political party on the schools, there has been little discernable change in the extent to which the union continues to set policy in the schools which is highly favorable to the union membership. For what has happened is that the political party has only been able to partially rearticulate the structure of authority affecting the schools. The party can influence a majority of school board members and the superintendent; however, it cannot influence the union leadership. Consequently, given the considerable degree of authority possessed by the union within the schools and its ability to withhold teachers' services, the system of union rule continues to prevail in the schools. The political party also is restricted in the degree of effort it can exert toward curtailing the teacher union's policy of aggressive pursuit of its self-interests because of the close ties between the party and organized labor.

The final point to be made about the rearticulation of the schools with the political party is that the party has proceeded with moderation, for the most part, with an eye toward maintaining the appearance of separation between the schools and politics. Such a strategy is, of course, dictated by the strong degree of public support for such a separation. Yet, the strategy is also designed to avoid responsibility on the mayor's part for the conduct and outcomes of the school system. Thus, despite the fact that the mayor clearly imposed settlements on the school board which have produced a budgetary deficit approximating $100 million, the mayor is not widely perceived as responsible for the deficit. He merely served as a mediator at the request of the two stalemated parties. Accordingly, even though there is strong evidence suggesting the mayor's dissatisfaction with the financial consequences of the settlements, the mayor nevertheless has managed to reap political benefits from the situation. To the union, he is the producer of the benefits in his role as highly persuasive mediator. To the public, the mayor is the producer of labor peace. This indicates one more aspect of Mayor Daley's legendary political genius. It also indicates, however, that even Daley was unable to come up with a means of coping with the teachers' union.

With regard to the process dimension of union rule, it was stated that union-rule bureaucrats would display a much higher degree of self-interest than their reform-rule and machine-rule counterparts. What makes the difference is the establishment of the union within the bureaucracy as a legitimate organization. Thus, it was seen in chapter 2 that under each of the three forms of urban governance a different type of beneficiary emerged. Each beneficiary, in turn, sought to restructure the schools so that it became a primary recipient of benefits to the exclusion of other beneficiaries. However, the machine-rule and reform-rule bureaucrats were limited in the extent to which they could alter the schools to their advantage because their self-serving activities lacked legitimacy. The political party had its way with the schools primarily on a basis of force. The reform-rule managers could only alter the schools to their advantage by contending that an increase and expansion in the professionalization of the schools was to the advantage of the clientele of the schools. Unions need make no such claims, although it is obviously to their advantage to do so. Unions are designed for the express purpose of increasing the benefits acquired by their membership.

The extent to which the teachers' union has been successful in becoming a primary beneficiary of the schools can be seen on virtually every page of the contracts reached by the school board and the union. Yet, what is of particular interest is the finding that the development of union rule in the schools actually underwent two distinct phases. Essentially, the two phases can be distinguished in terms of the extent to which the union pursued its self-interest. Thus, we termed the earlier phase as a moderate form of union rule, and the later phase, during which the union leadership began to display a much higher degree of self-interest on the membership's behalf, was referred to as a fully developed form of union rule.

What is noteworthy about the leadership during the moderate union-rule period is that while it experienced far fewer external conflicts, internally the union leadership faced continuous conflict, as several factions within the union expressed a variety of dissatisfactions with the leadership's performance and objectives. In effect, the moderate union leadership sought to serve as a go-between, not only serving the interests of the union membership, but the interests of all the other school beneficiaries as well: the political party, the school board and management, and even the school children to some extent.

Thus, the negotiating style and contracts approved by the moderate union leadership proved to be a constant source of tension within the union. The moderate leadership continued to oppose use of the strike tactic even after it had been shown to be highly effective in terms of increasing membership benefits. The moderate union leadership tended to accept the school board's financial limitations as a limit on what the union would seek, rather than demanding more and driving the board into deficit budgets. The moderate leadership also accepted the political party leadership's decision as to whether or not it would intervene on the union's behalf, rather than striking and thereby forcing the party leadership to intervene. Even the school children appeared to form a part of the perceived constituency of the moderate union leadership. The early union leadership publicly presented the union as bargaining on behalf of the school children as well as the school teachers.

However, such statesmen are rarely honored in their own communities. After six negotiating sessions, the moderate leadership was ousted from office by a coalition of teachers from within the leadership's own union party. The new leadership of the teachers' union immediately set out to alter the union's prevailing pattern of conflict. Under the fully developed form of union rule, a considerable amount of external conflict developed, but virtually no conflict remained within the union. The union now bargains exclusively on behalf of the union membership. It no longer accepts either the school board's fiscal constraints or the political party leadership's intervention preferences as legitimate considerations in determining a course of action. Even the school children now rarely appear in the union leadership's rhetoric. Since it is the union membership which elects the leadership to office, this type of behavior is obviously much more well designed to produce internal stability and hence continuity in office. It is, therefore, not surprising that the new union leadership has not even been contested in the union's last two elections.

While the two phases of union rule in the schools are interesting in themselves, they also are useful as a means of explaining how the teachers acquired the right to collective bargaining. Given the modest objectives and cooperative values of the early union leadership, the political party leadership's decision to support the teachers' quest for bargaining rights must have been partially based on the view that the teachers could be brought into the city's political establishment at a moderate cost in resource redistribution and conflict. As the early events bear out, such an assessment was highly accurate. However, with the fall of the moderate union leadership, the party leadership's strategy collapsed, and since that time the party leadership and others have had to pay a high price for their gamble in creating a Chicago-style form of union rule.

With regard to the set of actors occupying the bureaucracy during union rule, we made the following propositions. Union-rule bureaucrats would be more partisan politically than reform-rule bureaucrats, possessed of interests beyond their bureaucratic affiliation, and more inclined to regard unilateral managerial influence as illegitimate. In contrast to machine-rule bureaucrats, union-rule bureaucrats would display a more independent form of partisanship and be less tied to a political party, while regarding unilateral managerial influence as more illegitimate.

The propositions were confirmed; however, once again, the two phases of union rule through which the teachers' union passed significantly affected the extent to which the propositions were confirmed. In general, it may be said that during the earlier, moderate form of union rule, the propositions concerning union rule's differences from reform rule received strong confirmation, whereas differences between union rule and machine rule were not as clear. However, with the advent of the fully developed form of union rule, the differences between union and machine rule became much more apparent, thus strongly confirming both sets of propositions.

Once the Chicago school teachers acquired collective-bargaining rights, their level of partisan political activity increased significantly. However, to a great extent, the teachers' union became a component of the local political party. Indeed, the union's newspaper during the years 1967–1972 often read as though the staff belonged to the political party rather than the union. It was not uncommon to find feature stories and editorial commentary concerning Mayor Daley's activities, particularly as they involved education. After each collective-bargaining session, the mayor received lavish praise in the newspaper for his support of the teachers. The leadership of the union went so far in 1967 as to announce the formation of a bipartisan teachers' committee for Mayor Daley's reelection, and in 1971 the leadership announced that the teachers' union was joining the All-Chicago Labor Committee to support Daley's reelection efforts. All of this activity in support of the mayor and the political party must have come as a shock to those older union members who remembered when the union had been in the vanguard of the city's reform movement. The changes in the political orientation of the union following the grant of collective bargaining were indeed pronounced.

No less significant a change in the political orientation of the union occurred after the leadership of the union changed hands in 1972. From that point onward the union no longer endorsed local candidates for office, and the union newspaper rarely contained coverage of the mayor or the party. Indeed, during Mayor Daley's 1975 primary election campaign, only one oblique reference was made to the election in the union newspaper. This is not to say, however, that the teachers' union became less politically involved after 1972. What had changed was the union leadership's perception of where the political advantages of the union as well as the union's leadership were situated.

Thus, the union newspaper began to carry stories extolling the virtues of the union's national president, Albert Shanker, and more attention was devoted to state and national politics than to local politics. The union, in other words, began to focus on the independent interests of the union, apart from the interests of the local political party. Given the different viewpoints of the two major political parties, the union persisted in supporting mainly Democratic candidates; however, it now did so for reasons of self-interest rather than party or mayoral loyalty. Thus, in 1975 the union newspaper endorsed Republicans as well as Democrats and independents as well as regulars, all solely on the basis of whether they supported teacher legislation and interests.

The union also became much more active politically following the change in leadership. In 1975 the union announced it was forming an independent political organization that would be financed by a portion of the union memberships' dues. The following year the union newspaper announced that the political subsidiary of the union possessed a war chest on the order of $60,000. This means that the Chicago Teachers' Union is one of the state's wealthiest political financiers. Inasmuch as the CTU president also is the president of the state teachers' union, the teachers obviously have become a major force in state politics.

As for the politics of the teachers' union within the school system, the later union leadership can be distinguished from the earlier leadership in the extent to which it regards unilateral managerial decisions as legitimate. It was characteristic of the early union leadership to seek an accommodation with management and the school board. The later union leadership typically seeks to engage the management and board in confrontations. Newspaper accounts of several of the later bargaining sessions report the union bargaining team accusing management of manipulating the budgetary materials to conceal funds, and charging the board with not bargaining in good faith. Significantly enough, even the political party's closest allies on the school board, who invariably support the generous settlements with the union, did not escape the ire and accusations of the later union leadership. Thus, the school board, management, and even the political party are characterized by the fully developed union-rule leadership as bearing interests which are antithetical to those of the union's membership. In this regard, then, the later form of union rule is much different than reform and machine rule, and it can be seen that early union rule bore characteristics which were a carryover from reform rule's attempts to present an appearance of united educational interests.

The Utility of the Union-Rule Model

The utility of a model can only be evaluated in terms of its purpose; a model may be useful for some purposes and less useful for others. The basic purpose in developing the model of union rule was to use it to determine the scope and stability of the changes that occurred following the grant of collective-bargaining rights to big-city public employees. By developing the union-rule model in terms which encompassed the basic dimensions of structure, process, and set of actors, we were able to determine how comprehensive the changes were. By comparing union rule to the two preceding major forms of urban government, reform rule and machine rule, we were able to determine the distinctive characteristics of union rule. Finally, by using the "who gets what, when, how" framework developed by Harold Lasswell, we were able to determine the relationships between the major actors in school politics for the purpose of assessing the stability of union rule.

Another means of determining the utility of the union-rule model is to compare it to other research that has been conducted in the same area. By and large, social scientists have not devoted much attention to public employee unionization. To the extent that the subject has been studied, there has been an excessive preoccupation with the fiscal consequences of public employee unionization. While there is no denying the significance of fiscal matters to today's financially hard-pressed big cities, the concern with finances to the exclusion of other major aspects of public employee unionization has tended to produce serious misunderstandings concerning the significance of public employee unionization.

One of the remarkable features of those studies of public employee unionization which have focused on the financial question is that they usually have concluded that unionization has not had a significant impact. The finding is, of course, not consistent with what we discovered about the financial gains acquired by Chicago's school teachers. The basis for the discrepency would appear to be mainly methodological. For what the other studies typically have done is to compare unionized and nonunionized employees' wages on a cross-sectional basis. Unfortunately, such an approach ignores the differences that existed prior to the cross-sectional comparison. Thus, some given unit may have had very low wages and then, as a result of unionization, made substantial gains; however, the wage increases still may not have equaled wages received in a different location by nonunionized employees. From the point of view of a cross-sectional study, which focuses on only one point in time, the conclusion would be that the consequences of unionization are trivial, and, in turn, that unionized public employees are not distinctive from other types of employees.[1]

Moreover, by expanding the scope of the consequences of unionization to include the standard contract areas of working conditions, security, and managerial and organizational policy, further evidence may be provided that alternative conclusions are warranted, both in terms of consequence and distinctiveness. It is, of course, necessary to also look at the units over a period of time in order to determine any consequences of unionization.

Since we have considered the scope and distinctiveness of union rule in the preceding section, it may be appropriate to reserve our concluding observations for a consideration of the fiscally focused studies of public employee unionization in terms of their shortcomings as regards the stability of union rule. It is proper to begin by observing that the concept coined in this study, union rule, is not supported by the fiscal studies. Studies of a cross-sectional nature generally have found no significant differences between union and nonunion employee benefits. More recent studies of a longitudinal type have found greater differences, but the increases in benefits gained by the union employees have tended to level off after the initial bargaining sessions. Thus, rather than union rule constituting a new form of urban governance, it amounts to a novel development of a temporary and insigificant nature. The zeal with which unionized employees pursue benefit increases slacks off, and the public purse, after all, has its limits, as the purse holders have their limits of tolerance.

This may be true as far as it goes, but the point is that the assessment does not go far enough. When the financial limits are reached, then union rule's fiscal limits are necessarily reached too—although as we saw in the Chicago situation, deficit budgeting is one means of exceeding the limits. Yet, what we have tried to show is the comprehensive nature of what we chose to call a union-rule form of government. The union we examined made considerable headway in a number of critical areas, so that management, the governing board, and the political party and elected city officials no longer are able to set policy unless the policy is consistent with the union's objectives. This measure of control is what gives union rule its distinctiveness and its significance. Even when the wage agreements begin to take on a moderate nature of incremental increases, the radical characteristics of union rule will remain intact. The union will still possess the means of controlling the public organization, and thereby turning what had been, prior to union rule, a public agency into an agency principally serving private interests.

What has to be asked, then, is what are the means by which elected public officials and their delegates, agency management, can regain control of a city's public agencies once control has been assumed by the unions and written into a collective-bargaining agreement? What are the incentives for public officials to attempt to regain control? Some intense public pressure is probably necessary to induce a desire for change. Yet the union-rule revolution has been a quiet takeover, as the paucity of academic research and interest in the matter attests.

The media also have paid scant attention to the changes. With the big cities moving toward becoming what Norton Long has referred to as "reservations for the poor," there is even more reason to believe that union rule bears the hallmarks of an enduring form of urban government.

Note

1. At its 1978 annual meeting, the Midwest Political Science Association convened a panel on the "Impact of Public Employee Unionization on the Cities." Two of the three papers presented focused more or less exclusively on salary increases, with one study using a cross-sectional and the other a longitudinal model. Neither study found public employee unionization, as they had narrowly conceptualized it, to be of much consequence. Both papers provided bibliographical material which supported their findings. See, Russell L. Smith and William Lyons, "Public Sector Unionization and Municipal Wages: The Case of Fire Fighters, and Richard C. Kearney, The Impact of Police Unionization on Municipal Budgetary Outcomes, papers presented at the Midwest Political Science Association Annual Convention, Chicago, April 1978.

Index

About the Author

William J. Grimshaw attended and taught in the Chicago public schools about which he writes. He received the B.A. degree from the University of Chicago and the M.A. and Ph.D. from the University of Illinois, Urbana. From 1973 to 1977, Grimshaw served as an aide in the area of education to Illinois Governor Dan Walker. The author currently is teaching political science at the Illinois Institute of Technology in Chicago.